IRON EAGLE MUM

by

Dorine Mwesigwa

Copyright © Dorine Mwesigwa 2017.

Published by Dorine Mwesigwa and Action Wealth Publishing.

ISBN-13: 978-1977897183
ISBN-10: 1977897185

All rights reserved. No part of this publication may be reproduced or distributed in any form or by any means without the prior permission of the author and / or publisher.

The material in this book is provided for educational purposes only. No responsibility for loss occasioned to any person or corporate body acting or refraining to act as a result of reading material in this book can be accepted by the author or publisher.

Consulting, Editing, Interior design, and Preparation for Publishing by ActionWealthPublishing.Com.

Dedication

I dedicate the book to my parents Mr Geddy Mwesigwa and Margaret Mwesigwa and my five children. Marcus Mwesigwa, Valerie Milva, Melvin Edgar, Myles Hoppert, and Mariah Hoppert. My brothers Trevor Goldman Skibba, Brian Mwesigwa Arnold Conrad, and my sisters Olga Mwesigwa and Virginia Mwesigwa.

Acknowledgements

I acknowledge the two great professors that I met during my University journey who motivated me and made me start believing in myself again. Professor Dr. Martin Kessler was a great influence in my life. I regained my confidence and belief in myself through his lectures and motivational comments at my time at the Bonn University.

During this time, I was at my lowest point and nobody knew this, but I was able to succeed because of him. Professor Dr Neil MacDonald, who lectured me through my Bachelor's degree at the University of Roehampton and believed in me on my behalf, which enabled me to acquire an excellent Honours degree in Theology and Religious studies; that was a dream come true because, being a full-time mother, full-time wife and full-time student was almost impossible, but his faith in me helped me obtain those results.

Last but not least, I would like to acknowledge my current coach Geoffrey Semaganda, whom I met at a point in my life when I saw no hope and certainly no light at the end of the tunnel and everything looked bleak. He held my hand and walked with me on this challenging journey to this point of having successfully completed this book. He is the reason why I am a smiling Author. Through him I can hope to change lives. That has been and still is my passion.

Table of Contents

Acknowledgements	i
Introduction	v
Chapter 1: Every Journey Begins with One Step	**1**
My childhood	1
The Young Mother in All Mothers	6
The Survival Journey	10
Chapter 2: Following Your Dreams Finding Your Passion	**13**
Chapter 3: Taking Big Risks for Big Rewards	**33**
Meeting a stranger who changes your life	33
Knowing you need to change	36
Feel the fear and do it anyway	39
How to always get the right help	41

Chapter 4: Raising Positive Kids in this Negative World　　45

Chapter 5: Managing through Hard Times　　71
　　Keep Your Head up no Matter What　　71
　　Focus on what you can control, not what you can't control　　78
　　Learn to Let Go　　81

Chapter 6: Children and Technology　　91
　　Be a Good Role Model　　91
　　Do your Homework　　95
　　Set Limits and encourage Play Time　　101

Chapter 7: A Healthy Mind in a Healthy Body　　111
　　Create Your Own Health Plan　　114
　　Eat Sleep and be Happy　　123
　　Go Out and Have Some Fun　　126

Chapter 8: Building Your Success Muscle　　131
　　Your Confidence　　131
　　Your Courage　　134
　　Your Influence　　141

Chapter 9: Don't Look for Mr Right. Look for Mr Right for You — 147
- You are not Miss Wrong — 147
- Miss Independent — 151
- It Takes Two Tango — 156

Chapter 10: Believe in Your Purpose — 163
- Clarify Your Priorities — 163
- Don't chase material wealth. — 166
- Failure is Part of the Experience — 169
- Appreciate the Journey. — 171

Chapter 11: It's Time to Become the Success that You Want to Be — 173
- Invest in your Self Education — 173
- Have a Mentor — 176
- Have a product to sell — 178
- Build a business — 180

Chapter 12: Unstoppable Mother — 183
- Have Faith — 183
- My Top Five Principals for Success — 184
- Dorine's Final Golden Lesson — 188

Conclusion — 189

Introduction

Life does not always pan out how we think it is going to. Along my journey I have been through many trials, heartaches and disappointments.

My story that will unfold throughout these pages, is a hard one to tell, but I know that my story is my way of reaching out to others and helping them move forward with their own lives, as I have.

I have come far, I have many emotional scars from my past, but I am determined to not let my past dictate my future. Walk with me through my story and together we will grow and flourish and find ways to succeed.

I will share with you my life, so that you will be able to use what I have learned in your own life to perhaps forgive yourself and others, and to learn to let go.

Let's walk together and grow together as there is no richer aspiration in life than to live a good life that we have created. A Mother Determined to Succeed will show you that never giving up, no matter how many times you want to, brings rewards and success and happiness.

Chapter 1
Every Journey Begins with One Step

My childhood

Every little girl, at some stage of her young life, plays with dolls, pretending to be a mommy. They dress their dolls, talk soothingly to them, play games with them, pretend to feed them and then tuck them into bed and sing them a lullaby. I was no different than these young girls. I cuddled my doll against my heart and sang her the same lullaby my mother used to sing to me, dreaming of the one day in the future when I would be a mother and sing this lullaby to my own children as I held them.

I would be a good, strong mother and

protect them from harm, and we would live happily ever after. This turned out not to be as easy as that little Dorine dreamed of. Walk with me, and together through the pages of this book, I will take you on the journey of how I felt I had let myself and my children down, again and again. And how that feeling of failure made me determined to succeed.

Take my hand as I will sit with you a while and tell you of my journey that began with a single step that led me through heartache, fear and redemption that came from the deep determination to be that person, and that mother that I dreamed I could be when I was just a little girl singing to her doll in a small room in an African country far from where my story would take me.

I never had a loving relationship with my father. My father did love us, as we were his children. How showed his love through providing for us and putting us in good schools to prepare us for a better future. However, he was a militant man in the Army during the regime of Idi Amin. He ranked as a Major and commanded great authority. He brought us up with an iron hand and gave us harsh punishments whenever we did something wrong, or had bad grades. He was not a lovey-dovey cuddly kind of guy, and he did not read us bed time stories.

As a child I interpreted this as him being an un-loving dad, but as I have grown older I realise that my dad actually did love me, and that this had been the best way he knew how to parent me.

My mother on the other hand was the complete opposite.

As my male role model, I suppose in looking back, that I never expected kindness from men. As an adult, I have come to terms with his treatment of us. I have accepted that this is all he knew, and just how he was.

Perhaps my acceptance of this kind of treatment was my downfall in my dealings with the men in my life in years to come. But you can't look back and blame everything on your childhood.

My mother was our saving grace as children. She was the opposite of my father, - the balance to his harshness. She was warm and kind and stood up for us children.

When I was at primary school my teachers told my mother that I was a problem child and unstable. They said to her that I was so bad at my schooling that I would have to redo the year. My mother was having none of this and removed me from the school and put me in a more tolerant school where I had some happy years.

I moved schools a few times, as my mother believed that all I needed was love and support. I have to admit though, that I was a difficult child and a problem teenager through no fault of hers.

When I finished school, I did so with such good grades that my father wanted me to go to University. I was very opposed to the idea, as I did not want to be tied down.

I eloped with a young man and left. This was supposed to be my salvation – I was living my life on my terms. But it was a horrible time. I fell pregnant, had no support, and with my head hanging low, I returned home.

Now, in our culture, it was very frowned upon to be pregnant without being married or having the father around. My father had to hide me until I had the baby.

It was an embarrassing and soul-destroying time but once I had had my baby, a change started happening in me.

My life wasn't just about me anymore. There was another life that I had to protect and support. The mother in me had woken, and it was to be my saving grace as a person.

I have to say, even with everything I was still to go through, those years were tumultuous.

I was 23, unmarried, had a baby, but had no work and no prospects of work. Things did not look bright for me. But I was a mother now, and I was determined that I would do right by my child.

The Young Mother in All Mothers

Most women when they are about to

have a baby think that being a mother comes naturally. Even the most seasoned mothers will tell you stories of how being a mother came as a shock to them, and how the reality was nothing like the fairy story that they had been led to believe.

They will then laugh and tell you that wouldn't change it for the world. This is because there is something so special about being a mother, and how it expands you and deepens you as a woman, that no amount of sleepless nights, dealing with teething, tantrums, school dramas and teenage years would ever take away one iota of all-consuming love for your children.

They hold your heart in their hands, and whilst you would walk through fire to protect them, that is not always possible, and those times that you can't will break your heart in such a way that it never can be whole again. But from broken hearts come fierce determination to succeed and change. A mother will move mountains for her children.

But a young mother knows none of the angst that loving a child and not being able to protect them brings. She knows nothing of the torment of not being able to protect your children against the harshness of the world. She knows only of soft cooing and whispering and lullabies, of warm skin and tiny fingers. It is this young mother that believes in the beauty of the world, that believes in the magic of life that we have to find and hold onto throughout the years of our motherhood.

That young mother's innocence and belief will be the light that drives the fierce mother to fight for her children. We need to protect that innocent young mother in us because she is the lighthouse that keeps us away from the inner destruction of doubt and self-recrimination.

No one can succeed at everything. Everyone fails at something. The people that make it to great places in their lives are those that got up when they fell down, that found the inner mother in themselves and never stopped believing in the possibility of a good tomorrow, no matter what today held. To succeed you have to accept failure as part of life and use it to push yourself upwards until your head breaks through the surface of the water that threatens to drown you. You must see the lighthouse beacon and hear the young mother in you singing the lullaby of your childhood. That sound will make you determined to survive, determined to change your life and determined to make a life that lives up to the expectation of the young mother within you.

The Survival Journey

How do I know that the young mothers within is the saviour? I know because her innocent belief in what motherhood and life was meant to be, kept me going when I didn't want to keep going. Her belief in a good future for herself and her children kept me going when life was so dark that I couldn't see where to put my feet without falling down.

Looking back, I made so many decisions that I want to shoot myself for.

Let me tell you a secret about survival – the first of three steps is deciding that you have had enough of what is happening. The second step is make a change and move on. The third and equally important step is forgiving yourself for your past mistakes. That is how you survive and become a better, wiser person. Guilt, anger, resentment and wishing you had done things differently will not get you anywhere. They will keep you trapped in the past and you will not grow.

I made terrible choices in my life because I was stubborn and headstrong. But I survived those choices because I was stubborn and headstrong. That is the paradox of who I am, and why I am here writing this book.

I need to share my story with you in order to give you the courage to make the changes that you need to, in order to hear me when I say that you will survive.

Throughout my life I have been told I was unstable. A problem. Troubled. I have been poor, loved, hated, abused, lied to and misled. I have had my hope and trust used against me. I have been so down that I thought I would never be able to get up. But I did, because I was a mother. I was strong, and there was only me to protect my children.

I should not be here, but I am. This is my survival journey.

Chapter 2
Following your dreams

Finding your passion

When you have had your feet knocked out from under you, it is easy to just lie there, feeling winded, and not want to get up. That is quite normal. A certain amount of wallowing in your grief and anger is acceptable. We all deserve to rail against the unfairness of the world and shout "Why me?" for a while. Then there comes a time to dry your tears, and accept that while bad things happen in life. those bad things don't have to determine your life's course.

They are a detour, not a destination.

The moment you make the decision to get up, and not let what happened to you be the end of you, you have won. The rest is just trimming on the tree. Your mind is your strongest ally, and your strongest enemy.

You can survive if you are determined not to be beaten, not to give up. That is the greatest victory—and the greatest revenge. People who want to keep other people down because it makes them feel stronger have that strength taken away from them when the person they are trying to keep down keeps getting up, and refuses to let circumstances dictate who they are.

You will succeed as long as you refuse to let go of that young mother's belief in life. You will succeed as long as you refuse to fail. You will succeed as long as you hold onto the dream of a better future with both hands, and never let it go. You had a right to dream, you have a right to follow your dreams, and you have a right for those dreams to come true.

After I had my first baby, I knew I had to find a job, but there was nothing available. I was staying in my father's compound so I took the initiative and started a shop for the local people. It would have been a success, but too many people would take things, promising to pay the next day. This never happened, and my shop had to close as I couldn't carry the financial loss.

I was knocked down by this but not knocked out. I kept on looking for ways to make money.

I moved to the city, and there I found a place where every morning at 5am shoes were thrown together in a large pile and sold. I have always had a good eye for fashion, and I thought that I could make this work for me. I used to catch a taxi early in the day to ensure I got there early. I would choose all the imported shoes of a good style that looked like they had come from Italy, France and other continental places.

This is where determination to succeed kicked in. A lot of my friends from school had by this time secured good jobs in big corporations.

I put my embarrassment aside, and took my second-hand shoes to my friends in these big companies and sold them to them.

There they were working for MTN and other such prestigious companies and there I was, selling second-hand shoes.

It was hard, and humiliating, but I did it. It worked so well that within a month I was able to buy a little car so that I wouldn't have to go to and fro in the taxis. In that month I had also learned to drive, then applied for and gotten my driver's licence. One thing I know about myself is that if I put my mind to something, I will do it.

The car was a lifesaver, as I no longer had to travel in the dirty, jam-packed taxis anymore.

I could get to and from my clients in my own time. It was my first step to feeling like I was in control of my own life.

After doing this for some time, I got tired of doing this type of work. It was very hard, involved working long, long hours, and there is only so long that you can sustain that type of work. I had saved most of my money and told my mom that I had enough to open a shop back home. We could employ a manager so she wouldn't have to work in the shop.

I then went out to look for less strenuous work.

By a lucky chance, I met an old school friend who had recently opened an Internet Café. Whilst I had not gone to Uni as my dad had wanted, I had done some computer courses, so when my friend offered me a job, I jumped at it.

This turned out to be the start of a path that I think of as a detour.

This kindness my friend had offered me was just that – a kindness. He was a good boss and it was a good job. But through this job I met my first husband and what followed was a very dark time in my life. The dark time that followed gave me my next two beautiful children, but it was the beginning of a terrible part of my life, that led me to another country and into a life which was hell. I have come to see that those years of my life were a detour on my road to happiness. I am through it, but that realization has taken a lot of work, emotionally, physically and mentally, with a lot of very supportive people. I now know that I do have a future and, that the past is the past.

Sometimes in life, we go through detours that will try and drown our dream.

Situations will try and make us believe that dreams are a lie, and that there is only pain and sorrow in the world. Those are not the times to let go of your dreams. Those are the times to hold onto your dreams even tighter as they may be the only thing that keeps you from drowning. Without the belief that life has to have something better in store for you, than where you are now? You will never strive to make a better life for yourself. Without hope, people perish.

You have to know where you are going in order to find the path that takes you there.

You need to know what you want, what your dream is, so that you can change your life to make it possible. Everyone deserves a good life. Everyone deserves a life that brings them joy.

Whilst working at the internet café, I met a British man, with whom I became friendly. This developed into a relationship and he asked me to move to England to be with him.

I have never been one to shy away from risks, and although my friends were completely against the whole idea, and could not actually believe that I was even thinking about it, I wanted to do something daring. I wanted to take the risk. I was stuck in Uganda, working in a job that, while good, was not something I could do forever.

Against my friend's protests, I quit my job and packed up my things.

He met me at the airport with his nieces and nephews. Oddly, one of his nephews had a friend that I had gone to school with, so this made the initial meeting easier for us all. We bought some takeaways and went back to his house.

It was a pleasant evening of everyone chatting and getting to know each other. The man offered me the spare room and gave me a set of keys for it so that I could lock myself in until I felt comfortable. I took up the offer, as it was all very overwhelming.

Life went on happily for about six months, during which time we lived a pleasant life together and had become lovers.

I was always attracted to older men because I, I realised later, that I was looking for that father figure type of person that I had experiences as a child with my own father. This man was was 20 odd years older than me, and was in fact 2 years older than my mother.

I fell pregnant and had a child, and everything seemed to change around this time. He was increasingly obsessive, not letting me go out without him, and wanting to know why I wanted to go out and leave him behind. I wanted to get a driver's licence, but he refused to let me. He was always angry, and would often resort to hitting me.

I was so shocked the first time it happened. I refused to believe that it was anything more than a reaction on his part. I simply could not put the kind man I had known with this volatile monster that he had become. I tried to be a better wife, to not anger him, and to protect my child from his anger. By this time, I was pregnant with my second child by him, and I believed that every time he hit me, that it would be the last time. It was the only lie that I could tell myself.

I had nowhere to go, I was ashamed and alone. I now know that this is a common feeling for victims of abuse. Since then I have learned that there are many wonderful people who exist who want to help you. They do not judge you for why you stayed as long as you did, nor do they care that you did, Their only concern is that you receive the help you need in order to heal and move forward. Angels come in many guises, as I was to learn.

That was not a pleasant time. I slept little, ate little and was constantly on my guard so as not to set his anger off.

Shortly after I had come home from having the baby, I was sitting in a chair feeding our child. I had had a C-section so my body was in pain and I was tired. I can't even remember what it was that set him off, as by that time it seemed that everything made him angry.

He dragged me from the chair, hitting me. I managed to put the baby out of his reach but he he kicked me in the stomach. I felt something tear, and watched as blood started pouring out of me. I was in shock,

I couldn't believe that this was happening. All I could think of was getting to the phone to call for help. Dragging myself across the floor, leaving a trail of bright red blood in my wake, I reached for the phone and dialled the police. But as I got through, he pulled the cord from the wall.

In that moment I thought I was going to die. I wondered what would happen to my babies, and I knew that I had to hold on – for them. I wanted to die, I felt worthless, and useless. My husband hated me, and I was worth so little respect that he hit me whenever he got angry, which was often.

I was in the depths of despair, completely helpless as I lay bleeding on the floor. Luckily the call had connected, and even though I had not had time to speak, the police had been able to trace the call.

They came barrelling through the door to my rescue.

They detained him, called an ambulance and got me to a hospital. My babies were safe and I was taken care of. Once I left the hospital I was taken to a refuge for abused women. It was a shock to see just how many women has gone through what I had. It made me feel less alone, and more determined to succeed at life, and to succeed at being a mother.

I thought that this is where my story changed, where I started living the life of a strong, independent woman who would raise her children to know that no matter what happened, she would protect them.

I was not there yet, as my story was far from over. But let's take a breather and talk about what that bad relationship taught me. I blamed myself for many years. I felt like a failure, and mostly, I felt as if I did not deserve to have a good life. I wanted one so badly, but only as I started healing did I realise that I was the victim. I was not to blame. I deserved to have a good life. It would just take longer to come than I thought, and my suffering had not yet ended.

Before the next chapter of my saga continued, I had some good years.

I was given a temporary house, and then a flat in which to live. When offered a choice of neighbourhoods, I asked a friend which was the best one and chose that one. I wanted to be around people who lived good lives, in beautiful houses. People who sat around tables at dinner and laughed at each other's stories. I chose the neighbourhood that I thought would bring me peace, and for a while it did.

In that time, I spent many a sleepless night reflecting on the past years, wondering if I could have done anything different so that it wouldn't have ended the way it had. Was I at fault? Was I to blame? Did I deserve to have that happen to me? I eventually found some modicum of peace and I went about my life and spent time mothering my children.

I now know that answers to those questions, but it would take me many years— quite of few of them in a terrible situation—to answer.

No-one has the right to take your joy from you. If someone makes you believe that you don't deserve to have a good life, a safe life and a happy life, get as far away from that person as fast as you can.

Take it from someone who has been there, and knows that not all people in the world are good people. I know that some people take pleasure out of other people's pain and suffering.

Those people do not have the right to take your dream away. There are always going to be people like that in life, you have to learn to identify them and stay away from them. I took longer than I should have to realise that, and I used to beat myself up about how long it took me until I realised something vitally important: You can't change your past—and you can't let it dictate your future.

After a few years of living in Slough, I had a good routine going with my children and life had settled down into some sort of normalcy.

Just when I thought I was done and over with men, especially in the wake of my previous ordeals, along came my second husband. Now brace yourselves because much as this story may sound like something out of a book, but it is true.

One sunny summer evening I walked across the road to my local pub for a cocktail as I always did over the weekends to catch up with my locals. It was a very normal day with everybody jovial as usual. The men were drinking Stella Artois beer and playing pool, and some others watched football. My girlfriends and I were catching up what we had been doing during that long, hot week when I was startled by this big, tall man with a deep voice asking me if I could join him for a game of pool, to which I reluctantly consented.

We talked as we played and he told me he was on a two week's holiday in the UK and was staying at a hotel just a stone's throw away from my house.

At the end of the evening, we said our good-byes, and he joked that he would stop over for a cup of tea and an English breakfast, and indeed he did. That was the beginning of yet another traumatic relationship. However, during the first 5 good years of our 10-year marriage, he told me that he had prayed to God that, even though it meant travelling to the end of the world to find the love of his life, he was ready for the journey. The pub where we met had been called "Worlds End." I'd laughed when he'd told me that.

In my darkest time, when despair threatened to overwhelm me, I hear the faintest sound of the young mother within me, singing her lullaby, reminding me that I used to once have a dream of a good life for myself and my children. I grabbed that tiny speck of hope and faith and used it to drag myself out of despair.

I used it as a light to shine on the path ahead of me, that I hadn't even thought was there. I used that dream of a better life, the hope that it was possible and the determination for this detour not to be the destination of my and my children's life so that I could finally break free and start the journey to redemption.

Chapter 3:
Taking Big Risks for Big Rewards

Meeting a stranger who changes your life

Along the journey of my search for my passion, I came across many inspirational webinars that were being hosted by my current coach. I had been browsing online for a few years in search of a coach that would hold my hand along this path that I was walking, and I had listened to many different people. None of them had spoken to my heart and soul.

However on this particular occasion, while my current coach was hosting a webinar, something in my mind instantly clicked and I felt very strongly that the entire webinar was directed at me. It was as if he saw me, knew me and understood that I was in need of support and guidance. He invited his guests to email him after the webinar, and I did just that. I wanted to connect with him, as he seemed to have the answers that I was looking for.

There are times in life that you will meet people who will change you – for the better and for the worse. Meeting my life coach was a turning point in my life. He was one of the best ones.

Those are the type of people who can shake you up and make you realise that you have to make a change. They make you realise that they don't hold your answers, as you may think they do. That in fact you hold your own answers, and that they have been there all the time.

Everybody comes into your life for a reason. Some are there to teach you something. This has been a hard lesson for me to learn, because a lot of what I have learned from people, especially men, has not been good.

I think this is why I was sent a male life coach – it was the universe's way of saying that there are good, kind men in the world.

When you have been through the things I have been through with men, you become distrustful of all men. This stranger who spoke those words that went straight through me, needed to be a man in order to show me that there are bad people in this world and bad men, but not all people are bad, and not all men are bad.

Knowing you need to change

A few hours after I had sent off my email, I received an email back from this person I did not know, but only had heard of as giving life coaching.

He said that he would give me a call the next day, and he did as he had promised. Our conversation was so wealthy with many answers that I had been looking for so long, I felt with every cell in my body that this was a step I needed to take, and that immediate action was inevitable.

Here was this stranger, who didn't know me but understood that I was in a bad place. He helped me to realise that I needed to make changes in my life, if I wanted change to happen.

He encouraged me by saying that he would give me all the support that I needed, all I needed was to co-operate and be determined and to want to succeed. I was ready to learn, no matter what. I was determined to change my life.

I had had enough of my choices that I had been making, choices that had led me down dark paths and brought me pain.

I had had enough of who I had been. I knew I had the heart and will to succeed. I just did not know what to do to in order to become a success, and to succeed and survive the life choices I was making.

I was ready to learn. That is very important. You have to know that you need help, and you have to be willing to take the help. It is a hard decision, as accepting those two things means that you have to accept that you are not coping with your life right now.

We are so programmed to pretend we are okay.

We take on much more than we should, because we don't want to appear a failure. Let me tell you that failure is nothing.

Failing is human, but getting up again and again and refusing to let failure be your destination is how you change your life.

Wanting to be in a better place, wanting to be a better person, a stronger person who is living a better life means that you have to be willing to humble yourself enough to learn what you need to.

You cannot be arrogant and think you know the answers because, if you did know the answers, you would not be in the bad place you are currently in.

That is the bottom line. Accepting failure as a detour, and finding the right person to walk with you, encourage you and believe in you is how you take that second step to being where you want to be.

The first step is knowing you have to change your life, and being willing to learn how to do so and accepting you don't have the answers you need yet. Never give up hope that you will find those answers. The answer you seek is within yourself, you just have to find the right people to show you how to retrieve it.

Knowing you have found a person that can help you and guide you can change your life. It did mine.

Feel the fear and do it anyway

Deep within I felt was apprehensive, because, as being a single mum of four, without work and barely getting by, committing to this life coach was a difficult decision to make instantly. I did not know how I was going to afford to pay for the services. What I did know was that this if this was something I desired so desperately that I needed to pay a price. I did not know where the money was going to come from but at this moment, my desire outweighed the lack of money.

When you know in your gut that you have to do something, nothing is going to stand in your way. In my mind I was already determined that I was going to get all the coaching that was required to reach my desired goal of writing my book. I needed to tell my story, to put it out there so that it no longer haunted me in the way it did at the time.

I needed other woman to hear my voice so that perhaps I could reach them and stop them having to go through what I did. My story needed to be heard, of that I was sure. I had met someone who could get my story out into the world, and help me heal in the process. There was no other choice, I would have to find the money somewhere. It was a do or die situation for me. So I went for it without a doubt, without further second-guessing myself.

I made the change that would bring me to this moment where I would be sitting here typing up my story for you to read.

How to always get the right help

As I started spending much more time with my children than I had done in the past, it became clear that they had been seriously affected by the ordeals they had encountered. They were always angry, afraid, and aggressive. They would often get into unnecessary fights with other kids at school. But even in other areas I could see that their confidence had been knocked. I needed to help them recover from what we had lived through just as much as I personally needed to recover.

I then went on the hunt for how I could help my children. I sought professional help through psychologists and therapists that work with traumatised children.

Don't think that your children aren't affected by your bad relationships. You're their anchor in life, and when they see you going through pain, they hurt.

They feel helpless and this turns inwards making them angry at their inability to help. Any trauma affects children, even if you think they are too young to understand, they still pick up and absorb that anger, fear and negative energies that surrounds them.

My children needed help just as I needed help. If you are in that situation, my suggestion is to find someone that they feel comfortable being around, because they will not always just start talking to the therapist or psychiatrist that you take them to. That is the first step. The same goes for yourself – get help.

Don't think you can do this alone. Don't think you can heal alone. That thinking belongs to the victim you were, not the warrior you are striving to become.

You are not going to be judged for being weak for having gone through what you did. You are going to be lauded for being strong enough to get out and look for help.

Find the right help for yourself and your children. Whether it is after years of bad relationships such as mine, or after a divorce. Children feel the same anxiety, depression, and sadness when parents break up. They feel guilty and angry at both of parents for the loss of the family unit.

When you add an abusive father into the mix, they feel more guilt that they couldn't protect their mother, their anchor. Then they feel fear, because if their anchor is adrift, they are too.

Never underestimate the need to talk to your children about what has happened, no matter how much they don't want to and no matter how hard it is.

Feel the fear and do it anyway. Feel the embarrassment and do it anyway. Find the help. Find the answers. Find the future that waits for you. It is yours. It is good and you and your children deserve it.

Chapter 4:
Raising Positive Kids in this Negative World

Never has it been harder to raise children than it is now. That may be my opinion, and perhaps every parent in every generation said the same thing, but I believe that being able to keep your children safe and instil good values in them with all the availability the kinds of outside influences today is harder than ever.

Not only do you have to know who their friends are, you have to know who they associate with on social media. You have to watch what they watch on TV, YOUTUBE, and what movies and series they stream. You have to know where they are at all times because our world is not a safe place for children anymore. Home needs to be a haven. I know that is not always possible, which is why I have had to work through so much mother-guilt about it.

I now ensure that our home is the place my children can feel safe. I believe that this is where they will heal, and where they will know that their mother is always waiting for them when the world gets to be too much.

Parents have such a large role to play in the development of their children, long before social pressures kick in. The ideal world is one where the parents have those young years to nurture and strengthen their children's values and fill them with fortitude and self-worth.

The reality is that does not always happen. I know that first-hand, but I have stopped beating myself up mentally about it. The past has to remain in the past in order to forge a new future. If you constantly keep dragging the past with you into the future, you will never be rid of it and no one in your family will heal.

After you have made the break from a bad relationship, or a bad situation, spend as much time with your children as possible. Make it a special time, just you and them. You can take them places, or you can stay at home and watch their favourite movies. It doesn't matter what you do, just be there for them.

Let them see that you are okay. That what happened before is over and that you are together. This is the most important thing in the world. They too are survivors, and you need to help them find their inner peace warrior. A peace warrior is not just a fighter, he is a person in control of themselves and their lives. He knows when to fight, and when not to. He understands that the world is not a good place but that we can be good people in a bad world. You will need to restore their faith in the world, and in you. But mostly in themselves.

Be the support system that they need, but remember that no matter what they or you have been through, you are the parent. You are not their friend. They will have many friends, but one mother. Be kind but firm, and don't feel guilt trapped into letting them do what they want when they want.

Communication is the key to starting again. It will be hard, especially as a mother who wants to be perfect. Throw that illusion out of the window – there are no perfect people in the world. Everybody is fighting some inner demon, no matter how perfect they appear on the outside.

Don't be fooled. Every single person is carrying around some stone inside them. Therefore, talk to your children, explain to them that you feel horrible that they had to go through what they did, and that they had to watch what you went through. Tell them that you understand that they are angry, and may feel resentful towards you for not being stronger at the time, and for not saving them.

Humble yourself and show them your heart.

Then explain to them that you want the family to work together and help each other become strong, that you are a team.

Tell them that while you can't change the past, as much as you want to. Together you can create a good future and a good, strong, loving, supportive family, but it will need everyone to work together in order to make it successful.

I guarantee that you will meet resistance, especially if you have teenagers. Teenagers are tough cookies, and as hard on their parents as they are on themselves. Don't expect your words to be a magic wand. Let your actions going forward do the magic.

Be the mother you always wanted to be, starting now. Every day make the choice to be the type of person you want to be. This is not a cure all, it is a starting point for a better family life.

Set routines and boundaries for them. Children thrive when they know what the limits and boundaries of their lives are. It is like putting a fence of love around them. They are free to live and play within that fenced area, but they cannot go outside it. This is easier said than done, especially when your children and yourself have been through traumatic experiences, but keep at it. Explain to your children why you are setting boundaries, that perhaps you never did before because you wanted to give them everything they wanted to appease your guilt.

You are going to meet resistance. Expect it, accept it and don't let it deter you. Remember they are hurt and don't know if they can trust you to deliver on your promises.

I know I feel as if I failed my children, but that is not something I can change retrospectively. In everything I went through, I tried to protect my children. They are my heart and my life. I can't change what happened, but I can change today, and tomorrow and every tomorrow ahead of us. What I can change is the mother I am now, and the family we are now. It takes time—more time than you think it is going to take when you start out, trust me.

No matter how pointless it seems, or how much resistance you get, keep going. Keep moving forward and being the mother you want to be. It does not go unnoticed, even if you think it does. Children see everything, absorb everything and nothing gets put aside. They are sponges – for good and bad.

That is why getting yourself and them the best help you can be vital. It is a starting point for them to realise that being a victim doesn't mean they are weak, it means they and you were preyed upon by someone who was not mentally well, who has problems. And that is not their fault. Professional help means being able to put blame where blame is due. Some of it may be your own, but with the right help you can work through that.

Be willing to hear the hard truths. Steel yourself, because children are very good at throwing truth swords that pierce your heart. Especially if they themselves are hurting. Realize that this is the hurt and anger speaking, not the child. Be strong. Be determined to succeed. There is no greater quest in life than raising emotionally strong children who will go on to become strong adults capable of making it in the world on their own terms.

Raise your children with the goal of them becoming a better parent than you were. Having children is easy, raising them is hard. Healing them is heart-breaking work, but all of it is worth it.

Discover Your Children's Special Talents and Strengths

Every child has something that they are good at. It can be in sports, art, debate, academia, IT, singing, music or in many other areas. Help your child find their niche in life. Everyone needs to feel that they are good at something, perhaps even better even than other people in this thing. This gives them a focus and a platform to excel that raises them up from the other feelings they are working through.

Support them in this area, and take the rest of the children with you to support their siblings.

Be a family unit that the children learn to understand is going to always be there for them.

Go to the sports events, get your child involved in a choir, or a music school. Get your child extra tuition to help them excel in that area that they are good at. Foster a sense of worth in them. The greatest thing you can give your children is a sense of worth. Knowing that their hard-working mother and all their siblings would rather be at their art exhibition will mean a lot to them and make them feel that they are important to the family.

Develop a Can-Do Family Mantra

If you decide you can do something, or you decide you can't do something, you are right. It is your attitude and determination to succeed that will keep you going.

Remind yourself and your children that life is not easy, and that it can in fact sometimes be horrible, but that your attitude determines your outcomes.

Cultivate a solutions-based family strategy. This means not letting your children expect life to be a fairy story. It means letting them know that life is not always easy, but there is always a solution to every problem, if you are willing to find it and do it. The answers may not always be easy, and they may not be pleasant, but there is an answer.

Teach your children that no matter what life has put them through, or the obstacles they may face, they can count of you and their siblings to help them through. You can do it – together. No matter what it is.

A cord of one strand is easily broken but a multi-strand cord is strong enough to fell a tree.

Be a Can-Do family. Sometimes having a silly mantra that you use may drive your children to roll their eyes at you, but they will remember them. When problems arise you can say to them that you hear and understand their feelings and reservations about being able of succeed in this, but what is the family mantra? "We are a Can-Do family!" or "We've got this because we have each other" or "There is nothing Team Mwesigwa can't solve together!"

It will take time, especially if you and your children have gone through trauma, but start today and keep going. They may not have felt that they could rely on you or their siblings in the past, and this may cause scorn and resentment at you for trying to be a strong mother and attempting to create a strong family unit now. But be determined that you are going to make this work. Keep at it. Don't let the team down. Keep going, even when you want to give up.

You can do it, because I am doing it. Every day is a choice to keep doing it. Keep working on the goal. It is the most important goal you will set to achieve in your life. Wealth, a car, a house, international holidays are all so insignificant when you are working towards creating a strong family – a team.

There is no greater goal for a mother to

strive towards. It doesn't matter where you are now. No matter what you have been through, you can start working towards that goal today.

Cultivate Positive Beliefs

Our children are flooded with input from TV, social media and their friends. Most of their beliefs and interaction will come from what they see and read, which is why you, as a mother, have such a big job in order to be a voice that is heard in their lives.

They see adverts that tell them that if they look a certain way, or if their hair is straight, curly, black, blonde or green they will be liked and have friends. If their skin is light, dark, tattooed or pierced they will be looked up to. Or if they listen to this band, or this type of music they will be as successful as those musicians.

Children need role models, and as a parent it is our responsibility to ensure that they are getting the right input.

From the get go you need to tell your children that they are valuable and precious. They need to hear that they are perfect as they are, no matter what they read and see. You need to create a strong inner sense of self in them. No matter what age you are coming into this as a parent, you can start now.

Keep the lines of communication open. Keep talking and voicing your opinions.

You will invariably get a comment such as, "Oh Ma, you are so old school, you don't know anything about how the world works." That is okay – you are entitled to your opinion and to voice it. Be heard, you are the head of the family—be that.

Creating a positive self-image in a child means encouraging them in the areas they are good at, and supporting them in the areas where they're struggling. It means knowing who their friends are, and making your home a place for the children to gather in. That way you can see how the interactions happen, and use that to better your relationship with your child and their relationships with their friends.

Speak about your belief system, and make it the way the household runs. If you are a Christian, then that is how it is. If you are a Muslim, or Jewish, or Hindu, that is how things are run in the house. You are the head, and you will set the boundaries and systems in place for the family.

Children will invariably throw you curve balls; they are past masters at it. You will suddenly find that the child that had a bacon sandwich yesterday woke up and decided to be a vegetarian today. The child who sat next to you in church last Sunday now declares they are an Atheist. Work with your children in whatever they are going through, but stand your ground. Let them know that you accept their differences, but it doesn't change your beliefs. Tell them it is good that they are exploring other avenues, no matter how different they are to yours, but keep the family running on your terms. Be kind. Be fair. But be firm.

Creating positive children means that they need to know that you will love them no matter how many tattoos they get, or whether they believe what you believe or not. It allows them to grow around the core of a mother's love, and that that core anchor them in life.

Tell them you love them. This seems like an

obvious thing, but so many parents find it hard to tell their children those special words. Perhaps your parents never said it to you. But that simply means you need to deal with your issues on the subject and move forward. Children need to know that their mother is their greatest champion.

They need to know completely and totally and without a doubt she loves them no matter what, and will stand by their side through anything. Say the words.

Tell them how proud you are of them and celebrate their achievements with them. Comfort them in low times, and be the one they run to when things get bad. This does not happen overnight, especially if you have had a tough start as a family. Remember this is a process, not a magic wand. Keep at it.

Keep at the positive reinforcement daily. I read an article that stated that babies have to hear a word three hundred times before they are able to say it themselves. Perhaps children need to hear positive words just as many times before they start to believe it. I don't know for sure, but I do know that it is not easy, but it is worth it.

Everybody needs to know that there is at least one person who has their back – make sure your children know that that person is you.

Tell them you believe in them, you know they are going to be okay and successful and you are going to be there at their side every step of the way.

Give them something to believe in, and let that something be themselves. That is the greatest gift you as a mother can give your children.

Any parent with teenagers knows that their child will seem to go to sleep a loving child and suddenly wake up an angry adult.

Go easy on your teenagers, especially if they have gone through a bad time. Being the parent of a teenager is hard, but being a teenager is ten times harder. They are trying to find their feet in a world that constantly tells them they are not good enough. Social media throws hundreds of images, stories and words at them to make them feel inadequate. Be the positive in a negative world for your children. Be the one who they know always believes in them, no matter what. Be the one who always loves them, and who wants what's best for them.

Keep positive reinforcement as part of your daily skill set. Speak of good things that have happened, and find common ground interests that you can spend time discussing.

Reach out, and bring positivity into their lives. There is already enough negativity around.

How to Always Get the Right Help

I think the Americans have it right. Perhaps this is just what I pick up from the movies I watch, but there seems to be no social shame in seeking professional help.

I can't understand why in some other countries it is seen as a weak thing to do. By getting a trained professional to help you, you are being stronger and smarter than trying to sort out your issues and your past pain alone.

My advice is to find a professional person who has the right knowledge and experience to help you and support you as you start this journey towards your good, new future.

Professionals have a great deal of experience in dealing with the traumas, hurts and problems you are or have been through. They have dealt with them before and have studied them in order to be able to help you

find solutions that will suit your personality type, your problem and your family.

It is also good to be able to speak openly to someone who you know is not going to either judge you, or repeat your story to anyone else. There is a freedom in being able to tell your story in its entirity to someone.

I have found speaking about what I have been through has been a big part of my healing.

There are many Psychiatrists, Psychologists, support groups, life coaches, and such like that you can speak to. If necessary ask around, or ask your doctor, or Google specialists in your area of need. Get help.

I know we all think we can do this alone, but you can't. You need to get help in order to fully face whatever you have been through and to be able to plot a course for healing and discovering a better future. This goes for you and your children. Whether it is a divorce, or a trauma that has befallen you, know that it will have affected your children. Don't think they are okay as they are better at hiding hurt than adults are. It will manifest in the ways I spoke of at the beginning of the chapter – low self-esteem, getting into fights, running with the wrong crowd, withdrawal, anger and verbal outbursts.

Get the right help for yourself first. You can't help your children if you are not strong. The path is a long one, but keep on it. When you understand your past and make peace with it, you will be better able to help your children come to terms with it too. Then together you can work towards creating a new life together.

Often later on, family sessions are a good idea, as this gives the children a platform to voice their anger, concerns and problems in a secure environment. Know that you are going to hear things that will hurt, but hurting for your children is part of being a parent. Helping them heal and then experiencing our own healing in the process is the greatest reward.

Be strong, be positive and be the mother you know you can be. This is your life, these are your children, let no-one take that gift from you.

It might you are experiencing an emotional storm in your and your family's life at the moment, or you may have come out of one that has left you all feeling bruised and battered.

When I came to Germany, not knowing the language was a huge barrier for me to the extent that I almost lost my children to the government. What happened was that I was not able to communicate as everybody spoke German, hence I was not able to get anything done. I missed all the doctor's appointments and parent's evenings, and I was not able to read the letters that came to me through the post. In the eyes of the state I came across as this negligent mother who did not look after her children and their needs. So Jugendampt, which is the equivalent of social services, summoned me to court in in what would be a process of taking my children away from me. I was not provided with a lawyer as it was very short notice, so all they had was a translator. Nevertheless I defended myself and won the case and kept my children.

Know that you have it in you to hold on because the sun is coming out. You will feel the warmth of success, if you keeping moving forward towards your goals.

Chapter 5: Managing Through Hard Times

Keep Your Head up no Matter What

Moving to a different country, not being able to speak the language and everything my children and I went through there was one of the worst ordeals that I have ever encountered.

The language barrier turned out to be my greatest confidence knocker. Even though I am educated, being in a country where I didn't speak the language made me feel like I was the most ignorant, uneducated person on the planet. I did not like feeling like that so I invested in some German classes so as to be able to communicate. After I learnt some German to get me by, my confidence sky-rocketed and today I am able to help my children with homework in German. You too can do it. Confidence can be learnt

There are situations and times in your life that make you want to curl into a ball and hide from the world forever.

Life seems to be too big to handle, too horrible to cope with and situations seem too impossible to change.

That is where people resort to drinking or taking drugs. This is where depression and despair happen. I was so depressed at this time in my life that I took to binge drinking, just to numb the sharpness of the outside world for a while.

I soon realised that it was not changing anything, and hiding from the world in a bottle was not going to solve any of my problems.

No matter what, keep your head up. Don't let situations get the better of you. We all go through times when we are knocked down in life. You are allowed to lie there and kick and scream mentally about how unfair life is. But then get up. Get up and make a promise to yourself that you are going to change the situation, no matter what it takes.

Make a promise to yourself that you are going to succeed and move forward because you are worth it, and no person has the right to steal your joy or your happiness.

I am not going to focus on the details of what we went through while I was married to my German husband, as this book is about using pain and bad situations to catapult you into making changes in your life. Dwelling on bad details, and rehashing them just keeps the past in the present.

Suffice to say that we all came out of that relationship traumatised, and it is going to take a long time for us to heal, but I make the decision every day to keep my head up and keep moving forward.

When you have gone through trauma, no matter what it is, you feel beaten, deflated and alone. I am here to tell you that no matter what emotional pain you are in; you are not alone. Reach out to your family and friends, reach out to professionals, support groups and others who have been through the same or similar experiences, and get help.

When I speak to people who have been divorced they have heart-breaking stories of despair. With so much divorce happening, it has become commonplace. Do not think that your pain is insignificant.

All pain you feel is relevant and deserves healing. NO matter what your story is, if you are reading this book, you are looking for answers to help you heal your pain. I see you, I see your pain and I can tell you that healing is possible.

I can tell you that a happy future is possible. Just keep your head up and keep moving forward. Even if it is just one small step a day, don't stop moving.

If you have been so beaten by your experiences that you don't feel you can face the world, start by inviting a friend over for coffee. Perhaps next week you can meet that friend at a café, or go for a walk in the park. Push yourself forward a little every day.

I know how hard it can be, when you are so weighed down with the pain of your situation that you can barely breathe. When everything you do is just about more effort than you can summon. However, if you try to do something every day that pushes you forward, you will be surprised at how far you go in a short space of time.

Connect with people, make the effort to move forward because you are worth it.

As a mother it is always harder to wallow in your pain, as your children still need attention. There is school to take them to, sports, and extramural activities. There is homework, projects, and social activities they want to go to that takes effort on your part to get them to and from. There are meals that have to be made, clothes that have to be washed and ironed, housework, shopping.... The list is endless. When you are in despair, these things seem like mountains. Children can be your saving grace as these are all things you simply cannot avoid doing.

Therefore, you have to drag yourself up

and do them, but the little gem of having them is that it forces to focus on your life and its needs, and gives you time to start healing. You can immerse yourself in day to day necessary activities, and these can be the forward momentum that will get you to the place where you start healing.

The best way to overcome the past is to go forward, head up, chin up, looking life in the face and saying, "This is not going to be my story, this is going to be the start of my new story. I am going to succeed and be happy again."

You deserve to be happy. I know for a long time that I didn't feel as if I deserved to be happy. I couldn't understand why all these bad things were happening to me.

I felt victimised by life, as if it had it in for me. Only through working with professionals did I come to realise that bad happens to everyone in different forms, and while you can't control it, you can use past bad experiences to make yourself stronger, wiser and more determined to never put yourself in that experience again.

You can't change the past but you can shape the present and the future.

Focus on what you can control, not what you can't control

When you go through emotional pain, it consumes us. It is as vocal in demanding attention as physical pain is, and often lasts a lot longer.

Because it is so demanding of attention, it is easy to lose yourself in it. It almost becomes a companion. Holding onto it is easier than letting go of it. It is the reason you are like you are. It's the reason your life is a mess. It is the reason you can't work, and the reason you can't do anything except hide yourself in it. While that is true at the beginning, there has to come a stage where you let go of the pain. It is hard to do, as it often becomes a crutch for us to not move forward or make changes in our lives.

I have heard women say "My husband left me for his secretary five years ago and my life has been a mess since. I can't move forward as I am in so much pain." They can move forward, but it is often easier to blame the past, and use it as an excuse not to make changes, to not let go and move forward. If is scary to move forward, but it is exhilarating because you get to make the choices in your life. You get to forge the path to the future you want.

Don't let the past hold the future ransom.

Change what you can change, and let go of what you can't change. Let me tell you that the only thing you can change is yourself, and your mind-set. Everything else will change once you have renewed your mind, and rewired it from being a victim of life to being a champion of life. You are the pilot of your plane, the captain of your ship, the driver of your car – go wherever you want to. Your life's path forward is up to you.

Make good choices, ones that will benefit you and bring you and your children happiness.

You cannot change other people. You can only be an example to them and bring change to them in that way. The only person you can change is yourself. The only mind you can change is yours. The only life you can live is yours.

There are so many things in life that we cannot change and wish we had, especially the past. Regret is the greatest thief of happiness.

Wishing the past hadn't happened doesn't make it go away. Wishing your life was different doesn't make it different.

You deciding to let go of the past and move forward is what makes your life different. Do I wish I hadn't climbed that plane to England? Sure I do. Do I wish I hadn't married my German husband? Sure I do. But it doesn't change the fact that I did. I look at my beautiful children and am grateful that they came into my life, so I can't regret the past because it gave me them. For that I am ever grateful.

Learn to Let Go

Letting go sounds so easy. It has such a breezy sound to it, like a butterfly flitting away in the sunshine. Letting go is no butterfly, it is a hard and painful decision to make, and you have to keep making it. It doesn't just happen the moment you think that you should let go.

The pain comes back and it swipes your feet out under you when you are least expecting it. Then you start the 'picking yourself up' process all over again. Even though it does come back and does hurt you all over again, you have assessed it and see that every time it happens, it is slightly less painful, until you eventually feel only a twinge of pain. Then one day something happens, perhaps you see your ex-husband with his secretary who is now his wife, at a restaurant and you realise that you are okay. You realise that you wouldn't want to be married to a man who can treat a woman in the way he treated you anyway.

There it is – you have let go. In that moment of self-realisation that the present is better than the past, and that you have the future to look forward to, you have let go.

The negative has become a positive. You have moved into the next phase of healing.

I found that getting to that place took many years and still there are times when I want to weep in despair at what we went through. But then I remember that I have a future to plan for myself and my children—a good, happy future for us together as a family. I am in control of my life. I am a mother determined to succeed and raise children that will go into adulthood wiser for my mistakes, and better able to cope with life than I was.

The hardest part of letting go is forgiving. Women especially are not very good with forgiving. They move on, they create futures but they never forget, and seldom forgive. Let it go. It happened, so just let it go. Close that door and leave the pain behind it. By not forgiving you are constantly opening that door and letting the snow blow in and freeze you.

Forgive the person who hurt you, and forgive yourself for putting yourself in that situation in the first place, even though it was unintentional.

Those are easy words to write, and hard words to put into action. That is why I advocate getting professional help. I found that working with professional who had experience with people who have been through trauma, or pain, who understand depression or a myriad of other human conditions, will know some shortcuts to help you. They will be there to walk the long road too, and they will help you move forward then you don't feel as if you can.

Why I say forgiving yourself is so important

is that we so often don't forgive ourselves at all. It is easy to keep beating yourself up about the actions and decisions that put you in the situation you were in. But no one has the ability to look into the future, and you have to give yourself some slack. Tell yourself, "It happened. It was terrible. But I didn't make it happen. "

There are things that happen without your knowledge, things that happen when you back is turned, and as long as you can honestly say that you did not know, you can take yourself off the hook and forgive yourself.

Remember – you can't change other people's behaviour and you can't second-guess why people do things they do, and why they did things they did. Some people are just really messed up inside and use people as their outlet for their inner pain, turmoil and anguish. That is not on you.

Forgive, let go and move on.

When I found it in myself to forgive my ex-husbands, I found that I started looking at everything positively. I realised the idea that every adversity brings with it the seed of equivalent advantage. You learn from your past, you learn from your mistakes and you move forward, vowing never to repeat them.

The biggest growth in your life will come from adversity. Growth is hard, and adversity forces us to examine our lives, our current situations and yourselves.

You have to dig deep to find the strength to move away and move on. So many people stay in bad situations and relationships, because the change and the growth necessary is too big for them to cope with. That is why a good support system will give you courage and reasons to move on.

Learning to let go is something that should be implemented into every part of your life. Let go of any bad relationship that doesn't lift you up and make you feel better about yourself. Let go of old resentments, bad habits, bad thoughts, and especially let go of negative thoughts.

I cannot stress enough how big a part your mind plays in any change you are thinking or want to make in your life. If you think you can, you will. If you think you can't, you won't. It really is that simple. You have to be your own champion. Encourage yourself daily, and keep giving yourself pep talks. You can do this, no matter how hard it is.

You are precious, wonderful, beautiful, strong, resilient and a good person who deserves to succeed in life and be happy.

Make the decision to only absorb good things and people into your life. This doesn't mean that you must discard everyone that disagrees with you. If you do that you will stagnate, as being able to listen to other's opinions don't mean that you have to take them. But it doesn't mean that you must dismiss them either.

Everyone is brought into your life for a reason. Find the reason and you can learn the lesson and then let go and move on. Your past echoes into your present and affects the choices you make until you recognise your patterns and bring a halt to them. You know what I am speaking about, don't you? Everyone knows that one person that always seems to attract the very worst kind of partner for them—every single time! That is because they have not recognised their patterns of choosing people who are going to hurt them intentionally as that is what they expect. Perhaps it comes from having a non-loving parent, so there is no loving yardstick against which to measure men, or perhaps it is a feeling of low worth that makes these people choose who hurt them, so that they can reinforce that feeling of low self-worth and do the same things again and again.

If something keeps happening to you or you keep finding yourself in a similar unpleasant situation, you have to stop and ask yourself why that is. What are you putting out there that keeps drawing that type of negativity into your life? Where does that stem from? Once you answer these questions, only then can you break the cycle and let go.

You have to let go to live free, and you have to forgive to be able to let go. I know you can do it. You are here because you need to hear this. You need to hear my story so that you can change your story.

Do it – make the change. Start today and

then you are on the road to a brighter tomorrow. Do it your own terms.

Always remember the three rules of moving forward:

1. Keeping your head up no matter what

2. Focus on what you can control, not what you can't control

3. Learn to let go

Chapter 6: Children and Technology

Be a Good Role Model

Every parent will tell you that your child watches and sees just about your every move. They listen and hear everything you say and will repeat it. This shows how much of an impact you have on your children, and why being a good role model is so important.

When little Jonny goes to school and something goes wrong and he releases a string of expletives, it tracks back to mom or dad speaking like that in front of him. The way we act as parents, and especially as mothers who, more often than not, spend more time with our children than fathers, is very important.

We spoke about bringing a positive attitude into the home in the last chapter, and this carries on from that premise, in that how we act directly affects and influences our children's thoughts about themselves, their life and to some extent, how they act and speak to others.

I have given much thought about how parents impact their kids through all the parents' actions. I started watching how parents acted around their children. More importantly, I started looking at how I acted, and what I said around my children. That was the biggest eye-opener, as I realised that I was not being the best role model that I could be.

I found that sometimes, as we all do, I didn't listen when my children spoke to me as I was busy doing something else. I found that I sometimes snapped at them because I was having a bad day, or I didn't actively engage in conversation with them about what they are telling me. These are small, common things, but I realised that by making these small changes, I could be a better mother and a better role model for them.

I then started working on myself to be the best role model I could be to my kids; I made a conscious choice that I was going to do everything I could possibly do to enable me to bring up healthy, brilliant, happy and fully recovered kids. I had to do some inner work on forgiving myself for making the choices that had led us to the place where my children were angry and emotionally traumatised. That is still a work in progress. But I reflected upon every area of my life that I had not rectified, and tried to make peace with our past so that I could move forward.

I tried to present myself to my children, not as a broken, beaten, weak woman, but as a human who had made mistakes, but had learned from them and was using the bad past to make a good future.

What I have learned, and it has come as a balm to my raw pain, is that by showing your children that bad happens in life but we can learn from it and move away from it. I showed them that you can overcome the experiences and use them to make your life better going forward. I resolved that as the only mum they were likely to ever have, I had better do a good job of it.

As parents we like to think that our children will all be okay as long as everything is around them is okay. While this can work, life doesn't always play out in that way. When bad things happen, as they did to my family, I felt as if I had failed my children as well as myself. Other people seemed to have it all together, and I was a mess. Looking at myself objectively, I think my children have learned a lot from me about what not to do, as much as how to come to terms with bad that happens. I can only hope that they now see a mother who is strong, and determined to succeed at creating a haven at home for her children, not just in where we live, but also in our cohesiveness as a family group.

Do your Homework

Although the German language was somewhat of a challenge, I decided to invest 12 months in learning German so that I could get involved in every aspect of my children's lives, especially helping with the homework which is all learnt and written in German.

I am pleased that I did, as it not only helped

with being able to assist my children in their lives and schoolwork, it aided me in being able to understand all the aspects of their lives in the time we lived in Germany.

I have implemented this thought process into all areas of my, and my children's, lives. If you want to know what is going on with your children, you will need to have knowledge of the things they are interested in and doing. If you want to have a say about their time on Facebook, Twitter, Instagram and other social media platforms, join them and get first-hand experiences of how they work, and what the dangers are. There is nothing more annoying for a child to have a parent telling them things about something they have no knowledge of, or only have second-hand knowledge of. Take Facebook for example – only once you are on Facebook will you see that sometimes you get friend requests from strangers. It is all very well teaching your three-year-old about Stranger Danger, but teenagers are more relaxed about things like that. But by knowing that these types of friend requests come along, you can speak to you children about them and explain why they should not accept a friend request from someone they don't know. Depending on their age, you can decide whether to go into detail about how sometimes they can be innocent requests from people who have seen their posts and want to be friends. but you can also speak about how sexual predators create fake Facebook pages to lure children into becoming friends with them.

While we are on the subject of social media, let's discuss age appropriate usage. Most social media is not age appropriate for pre-teens. The things they are exposed to and the openness of the platforms should be well monitored even in teenagers. While I am not advocating hacking your child's social media, just be aware of what platforms they are using, and who they are interacting with.

Giving a mobile to a young child, or pre-teen is also not a good idea. There is no reason they need one. This may sound archaic in this modern day and age, but everything a young child needs and wants to do can be done through a parent. Only when your child starts going out without you and other adults is it a good idea for them to have a mobile.

Converse with your children before any change is made. If you are going to get them a mobile have 'The Talk.' Speak to them about why they are now allowed one, what the parameters are and what the consequences are for overstepping those parameters. Setting ground rules means that everyone knows what is expected of them.

Get the right knowledge you need to enable your child to live within sensible boundaries. Whether it is the friends they see, the places they go or the technology they use. Do your homework so that you can speak from a point of knowledge, and not sound ignorant about what you are talking about, as this will give the children room to dismiss your advice.

Let me let you into a parenting secret: Knowledge is power. I know it sounds trite, but it is true. You don't only have to have knowledge of the technology and social media platforms, games, online games, online chats, internet sites and such that your children are going to be exposed to. You need to know who they are friends with, where they are going, who is supervising where they are and what other type of people are likely to be there. Parenting is hard work! However, when you have all this knowledge, you can educate your children wisely into the pros and cons of a situation, and give them the skills to extricate themselves from it, should it be necessary.

Always give your children a Free Out.

This is when they can call you from anywhere, at any time and you will not Mom them when you fetch them. This gives teenagers an escape route when they need it that doesn't come with a lecture about why they were where they were.

Being a parent and keeping your children safe is of paramount importance, and giving them a Free Out will allow them to call you should they find themselves in a situation that they shouldn't be in. Remember that teenagers will sometimes get themselves into situations that they don't want to be in, and knowing that they are not going to get a mom lecture about it, will possibly keep them from staying in that situation or place, and get them home safely.

I have found that being able to say no to something and being able to blame their "strict" mother is a useful tool for children, especially teenagers. It keeps them from having to do something that they don't want to, while not making them look like they are soft. I have never minded being the "strict" parent if it keeps my child out of trouble.

I don't need other children's approval, and while it is a good idea to foster good relationships with your children's friends, it is also good for them to see that your child and your home is a strong, safe place in which boundaries and people are respected.

Set Limits and encourage Play Time

Be kind, be firm and listen to what your children are saying, verbally and non-verbally. Sometimes it is okay to throw the NO Snacking after dinner rule out of the window and have a DVD, ice-cream and chocolate indulgence while you all cuddle on the couch and watch a mid-week DVD if one of your kids is having a bad day or week. Understand that they are sensitive and vulnerable people. Soft adults that feel things very deeply and life is not easy for them, so even though you have rules in your house, know when to break them, every so often. Give love and understanding, but don't allow your love for your children to make you always give in to them.

With younger children, and even with older ones, keep your boundaries strong. Set an allocated TV, DVD, or gaming time and stick to it. Know what they are watching, or what social media they are on. Know what games they play and what movies they are going to see.

Remember that age restrictions are there for a reason, and act accordingly. Now do all this while still maintaining a good, friendly relationship with your children. Yes, the balance is not easy. It is very hard, but you are the parent and have to be their unwavering plumb line that they can trust not to move.

Encourage other activities that don't involve a computer screen or a TV or a mobile phone.

Help your children develop their other talents, and spend time on learning what they are. If your child shows a musical talent, encourage it and help them develop it, perhaps by buying them a guitar from the second hand shop down the road with the promise that, should they still be interested in playing in six months' time, they can go and choose a new guitar then. This encourages them to work towards a goal, and sets milestones to achieve this goal. In all this balancing, regulating, supporting, educating and raising children, you still need to teach them good life skills.

What a privilege it is as a parent to be given a child to nurture into an adult. It can feel somewhat overwhelming at times, especially if the children have had traumatic experiences in their past but I believe with love, solidarity and support, anything is possible.

Encourage your children to do things outdoors. Even if it is going on a walk in the park together or a picnic, or taking a train trip to the country, do things together and encourage them to get outdoors. Very little beats the blues like the sun on your face and warm grass under your feet does. In winter, if you live in a cold climate, go ice skating, or find indoor activities that you can all do together.

Your ability to bring a good world into your life will make your children's own life view better. Travel if you can, expand their minds with the possibilities of what the world has to offer them. Take them to see new things. Even if they complain about it, do it anyway.

Children complain. They moan about how they don't want to do things. But once they are there and doing them, they change their minds, so don't let their gloominess stop you or you will never do anything. Going out together is a good way of bonding and keeps the family unit cohesive.

Have fun, whether at home or out. Make sure that there are counter balances to the checks that you have put in place. Let your children breathe a little. Give them safe freedom to just be kids sometimes. Forget that them playing in the mud or fishing in the stream down the road is going to bring dirt and smelly fish into the house – let them do things that are fun. Build table forts with your little children – you know the ones where you throw a blanket or two over a table and climb under it and pretend you are in a forest? Have a picnic under the table, your little one will love it.

Play with your children, no matter what their ages. Sometimes playing involves going shopping with your teenage girl, or getting your nails done and then going for lunch. Sometimes it means sitting through concerts of music you don't enjoy. Instead enjoy being with your child or children. They will notice that their busy mum is making time to be with them. She is making them a priority and they will appreciate it.

The counterbalance to setting rules is showing respect. Respecting that your children will want, and do need, space from you is something every parent has to come to grips with. It is not a rejection; it is that they need space on their own to just be.

Being a parent is a diverse job. You have to set rules and boundaries. But know when to ease up on them. You have to let your children have the space to grow, but monitor who they interact with and what they are interested in. You need to give them time alone. Get them to work at school, ensure they eat well, sleep enough, get exercise, feel emotionally secure and are strong enough to stand their own ground while still showing respect for their fellow family members, friends and elders.

Amazingly enough, mothers balance all this diversity.

Know the Value of Face to Face Communication

I discovered that a one on one interaction with each child is very important. Children are all different, regardless of whether they are siblings or not. Each one of them is affected differently by the same events and situations. Therefore, each child needs individual attention. Giving a child one on one time builds their confidence as well as their trust not only in me but also with other people in general.

Spending one on one time with a child, teenager or young adult shows them that they are important as an individual, and that you care about their personal needs, not just the needs of your children as a whole.

Not all your children, should you have more than one, will like the same things or want to do the same things. While I advocate together time as a family, I also advocate time spent alone with a child doing things they they like to do, or even just spending time talking to them.

This is a good way to gauge where they are emotionally and see what problems they are facing and offer support. I found that something as simple as baking with a child, or watching a DVD with them, or perhaps taking them out for a milkshake gives you an opportunity to catch up on where they are in their growth, and what areas they are finding interesting and what areas they are struggling with. A lot of parenting is simply about being there to listen.

There will be situations that you can't do anything about. Those are the hardest for a parent, because you want to fix everything for your children and make the world wonderful. Unfortunately, life isn't like that and sometimes all you can do is put your arms around them and let them cry. It is heart-breaking but they will know that you are there for them and will help them heal.

Being a mother is one of the hardest and definitely the most rewarding jobs on earth. Keep going, keep moving forward and don't doubt yourself – you've got this. You can do it. I know you can. All the heartache, tears, frustrations and feelings of failure will be worth it if you just persevere and keep going with the routines, boundaries, family times and one on one times.

It is worth it. It is necessary, and I know you will succeed if you are determined to do so.

Chapter 7:
A Healthy Mind in a Healthy Body

A healthy body promotes a healthy mind. Think of how you feel when you are ill – listless, un-motivated, tired and despondent. When you don't eat correctly, your body acts in the same way as when you are ill. By eating correctly, and getting enough nutrients and vitamins into your system, you keep your body functioning properly. Combine that with exercise and positive thinking, and you have the best balance you can have.

Good health will change your life. We are complex creatures, and a lack in one area directly affects all other areas. Taking a holistic approach to your mind, body and soul will help you balance your mental, physical and emotional well-being.

The first step is to eat the right fuel for your body. I am not going to advocate one type of eating plan, as I believe each person's needs differ. What I do advocate is that you keep a food diary for a week and also write down how you feel during the day. This will allow you to see if certain foods affect you positively or negatively. For some people, eating white breads or other items made with wheat makes them feel tired and listless.

This is because their body is using all its energy trying to digest a food substance that doesn't agree with it.

Become aware of what you eat. If you notice that you eat a lot of takeaways and fried foods, try changing that and see if it brings about a noticeable difference to your general well-being and energy levels.

For some people, eating meat makes them feel sluggish. For others, it is diary that brings on that feeling of being bloated, tired and fatigued.

Get to know your body and what it wants you to eat. Be sensible, and be wise. Your body needs food to function. It needs nutrients, vitamins, minerals and omega oils and a variety of other things that you are not going to find in your fried burger and fried chips. All things in moderation, especially sugars, fats and junk food. I would recommend cutting out refined sugars completely, and replace them with natural sugars from fruits, stevia or honey. The reason being that refined sugars are foods that cause inflammation, and are not great for your general health. They lower the metabolism and they also are the cause of heart disease, high blood pressure, diabetes and many other illnesses.

Create Your Own Health Plan

There are many different diet fads. All you have to do is Google search and you will be inundated with answers on what is 'the best diet plan in the world ' Every person is different, so every person has to find the right health plan for themselves.

Once you have created your food diary, you will be able to pinpoint foods that do not agree with you, and foods that do agree with you. While I am not a fan of diets, I do believe that there are general foods that benefit the body, and foods that are not good for anyone to eat often.

Try and incorporate low GI breads, instead of white bread. These breads digest slower in your stomach, keeping, you fuller for longer and allowing your body to use the energy from the bread more effectively.

Keep sugar to an absolute minimum. Sugar is a trickster – it gives you a quick lift and then dumps you further down than before you had it. Honey is a good alternative to sugar, but for vegans this is not an options, so natural alternatives such as Stevia, or Xylitol are a better option.

Add colour to your plate, in the form of fruit and vegetables. I don't understand people who say I don't like the taste of vegetables, as there are literally hundreds of different things you can make with them, and none of them taste remotely the same.

Vegetables can be savoury, sweet, cooked in soups and stews, tomato based, cream based, the list is really endless.

My children did not like vegetables,

however I have had to learn all sorts of different ways which to cook them and make them desirable for them. Be creative with your cooking, make it something that brings out your creative side. Cooking can help reduce stress after a long day, but you need to have an idea of what you are going to cook and how you are going to do it or it will become a chore. It's always best to involve the children whilst in the kitchen, that way you hit two birds with one stone; firstly they learn, and secondly they reduce on the cooking workload.

Plan healthy meals ahead of time. For example, spend half an hour on a Sunday afternoon, sitting in your favourite chair with a cup of tea and work out what you are going to do for the week ahead in regards to meals. This way you can shop once for what you need, and you will know that all the health and nutrition needs of yourself and your family are taken care of.

The unhealthiest meals are the ones we have to think of making on the fly because it is now 6pm and the children are grumpy because they are hungry, so you throw fish fingers and chips in the oven. If you prepare your meal plan in advance, everything will be taken out, thawed and ready to cook.

On busy days you can cook easy, healthy meals and save the fun, more complicated ones for day when you have more time.

Food has become an obsession. What you eat, how much you eat and what food you put with what food. People have forgotten two fundamentals that seem to oppose each other but actually don't. Food is fuel, and food is fun.

Many people give an excuse for eating too much under the guise of their love for food, however, in my opinion that is food abuse not love of food.

The love for food, for me, is going out shopping for healthy food items, coming back home and cooking from scratch. That way you know exactly what is going in your body. It's true what they say, "You are what you eat".

I know someone whose children refused to eat cauliflower and mash potato. So she dyed those two white foods the child's favourite colour – purple. The children thought this was the funniest thing and ate all of it.

Another trick for fussy children is backward meals. Yes, they get their dessert first, but if they don't eat the real meal it doesn't happen again. It is amazing how this and other simple games make food fun for kids.

Or you have an incentive that has them trying food they think they don't like at least once. Maybe an extra 15 minutes of TV time or staying up later than usual.

Perhaps they think they don't like a food but have never tried it. Get creative, moms, make food fun and you will find that even you get caught up in the fun of food. You have to be smart in the kitchen when you have young children, and learn all the healthy ways of eating for when you have teenage girls. Teenage girls suddenly become very health conscious and this is something you need to help them with, and still ensure that they are still eating enough of the right things.

Try new things. There will be things you all hate, but that bonds you together. Start a veggie garden. It doesn't have to be big. It can even be a crate on a balcony. Young children love to dig in the dirt and grow things, so let them grow beans, strawberries, spinach, tomatoes and easy fruit and vegetables that you can use to cook with. Imagine how proud they will be when the food they have grown is served to the family for dinner!

Try different healthy meal options. Try meat alternatives such as Quorn, soy, tofu, seitan. Get creative in your cooking.

Adding spinach to fried onion and mash potato is a great way to get iron into kids. Use the many, many celebrity chefs to persuade your kids to eat different foods.

Most children love pork sausage, but frying them is not a good way to cook them, so I throw them in the oven with a little olive oil and they cook even better than on the stove top. Bake where you can, and fry as little as possible.

Eating healthy is a necessity for your body and your well-being and definitely a necessity for your growing children. Make food fun.

Get the children involved in making food. Let them choose a meal a week, or let them cook or help you cook dinner. Baking with children is a good bonding exercise.

This brings me to another thing that all children should be doing – chores.

The Merriam-Webster dictionary defines a chore as a small task or routine that is done regularly. I like that. That is exactly what children should be doing. The elder children can wash the dishes, or help with food preparation. The younger ones can set the table and dry the cutlery. Make meals a family gathering right from the preparation to the cleaning up. Children need to have chores as it teaches them to be responsible for something, and gives them the chance to be proud of doing a job well.

I have no doubt that they will moan about having to do them, but ignore that and keep going.

Speak as positively about food, as you do about life, because I believe that a healthy mind goes hand in hand with a healthy body. I discovered that when I started speaking positively to the children, not only did they cheer up and ditch their fears, but they recovered a lot quicker than was expected. They were more responsive to others and to life in general. We could communicate better. If children feel nourished, in body and mind, and emotionally, there is little that can beat them.

I can say this because I have tested it on my own children. Healthy eating has had a very positive impact on them. They look healthier, stronger and happier. They deal with situations better and they sleep better.

We are better emotionally because we eat better. Who would have thought that something so simple could have such an impact on our day to day life?

Eat Sleep and be Happy

It's very important for children to get enough sleep, as this will have an impact on their performance the entire day, affecting work, play and definitely their attitude and mood.

We have spoken about how children need boundaries and routines to flourish.

Setting bedtimes for younger children needs to be part of this routine. If you are unsure of what the general going to sleep time is, ask the teachers at your children's school, or the parents of you children's friends and then adapt that to your own children. Why I say adapt the times, is that some children need more sleep than others and some less. You will have to gauge each child on their own needs.

Before lights out, have a calming down period. Half an hour usually is enough time.

In that time the children need to be in bed, but they can read, or listen to an audio book or quiet music. Keep stimulations out of this time, and you will find that your children go to sleep easier when lights out time comes.

Also, children who have a full tummy are more restful, especially if they have a full tummy of the right food.

Small children need an afternoon nap, even if they don't sleep but perhaps just lie down for a while to rest. This stops the four o'clock moans. When they get up give them a healthy snack. Some apple slices and a glass of juice and water is a good option. Their little tummies need filling more often than ours do and often the crankiness in small children is simply hunger that they don't know how to express.

Children will often wake up early, so ensure that they are going to be at a good time to help them get the required amount of sleep they need.

Without enough sleep, children will become lethargic, moody, unable to work at school and short-tempered with friends, teachers and parents alike.

Make sure you balance the routine with fun, or your children will feel as if they are in a military school and resent you for being too strict.

Just a Mom word here: at some time in your child rearing years, your children are going to go off at you about your rules, regulations and the standard barb of "why can't you be like so-and-so's mother?" will be thrown. Take it in your stride. Calmly tell them that this is how you have chosen to run your house and raise your children, because you feel it is the best way for you and for them.

Don't engage in angry exchanges. Be calm and stand your ground. That is going to be a challenge at times, but it is worth it.

There will be days when your children seem to be on some super energy potion and it is all you can do to stop them from running up the walls. Those are the times you need to engage with them, either lie down with them and read to them, or tell them stories of your childhood, watch a movie with them, go outside and play a game with them or take them out to the park to run off some of that energy.

Go Out and Have Some Fun

Speaking of getting out and having some fun to keep your children calm, you will have to do the same to keep yourself calm and sane. This mothering thing is not for the faint-hearted!

I have learned not to take life too seriously. This is something that has taken me a long time to do, as life, especially as a mother with four children tends to get serious very easily.

There are times when you have to take a 'momma break' and concentrate upon yourself and your well-being, because an exhausted, frustrated and despondent mother is not going to be able to give of her best to her children. She is going to be short-tempered and feel trapped in an endless cycle of sandwiches and homework, washing clothes and enforcing bedtimes. It is exhausting, which is why it is so important for you to take some Momma time.

You can explain to your children what you are doing, and it can be done in the house.

Use half an hour of time when they have

to play by themselves while you sit and have a cup of tea and read you book. Teaching children to play by themselves, or entertain themselves is a valuable lesson for them, and teaching them that Mum is also human and also needs a bit of down time will give them a new perspective of you. Children tend to think of parents as super-humans that have been put on the earth for the sole purpose of looking after them. While this is a lovely belief, and certainly for their very young years it tends to be true, everyone needs to learn respect for the other family members' role in the family, including their parents.

I believe that if I feel well then that will impact the other members in my family, so I make sure that I have time out.

I believe strongly that as a parent you need to have your own time with people your own age. Whether you join a book club, or a dinner club or a gym. Go out and interact with people with whom you can talk to about things other than peanut butter sandwiches.

I believe that it is very therapeutic, and emotionally and mentally rewarding for a parent and most importantly it is an anti-depressant. You will come back enlivened and happy to carry on with the day to day routine. Don't lose yourself in being a parent, because it is very easy to do so.

I lived that experience. I found that I was feeling frustrated, grumpy and was not giving my best to my children. "Work without Play makes Jack a dull Boy".

Once you have established your boundaries, routines, healthy eating, chores, fun times and sleeping times, your life will be easier as everyone will know the rules. Although you will guaranteed hard days when it all goes haywire, for the most part, it will help you by giving you a bit of breathing space during the busy years of raising children.

Feed the body well to enrich the mind and steady the emotions.

Enough food, love, activity and sleep are the cornerstones of good parenting. Your children will thrive within these boundaries.

Chapter 8:
Building Your Success Muscle

Your Confidence

Along the path of my life, I have had many challenges, and my confidence was severely knocked several times. These knocks would leave me feeling victimised by life, beaten, bruised and very depressed. I could never understand why I was going through these situations when everyone around me looked as if they were living the perfect life.

After a lot of wallowing in my pit of despair I learned the very valuable insight that everyone is going through some challenge in their life, even if they don't show it, or let on that it is happening. When I learned this, I just let go of the feelings of being victimised, and I realised that life can and of often is, hard. Then I told myself to get over it, put my mental fighting gear on and stop moaning.

I came to realize that every challenge that came my way knocked me for six and threw me into a pit of despair. But, after wallowing and feeling sorry for myself, I would find that core within me that refused to give up, that refused to let the situation get the better of me. Every single time I resolved to get up, stand up and move forward.

There is a famous basketball player that says the only reason he is a success today is that even while he failed time and time again, he refused to give up and be beaten. He got up, stood up and fought another round, another day and won.

When you accept that life is going to throw you challenges, and believe me, some of them whip your feet out under you, the thing to remember is to never, ever, ever give up. Giving up is not an option, as it will keep you in the same place for as long as you let it beat you.

Life is hard, but without hard situations and challenges, we would be complacent people and would not bother to grow. The reason we are on this earth is to grow and learn and to love.

Accept that life throws curve balls at everyone. But the choice whether you lie down and wallow in your misery, or get up and decide to use that has happened to make your life, your children's lives and your future better, is yours. That choice is yours.

Make the right choice, choose to fight, to survive and decide to grow from strength to strength, learning what you can from every step of the lessons that you are given.

Making this choice as made me the strong and confident person that I am today. I thrive on challenges and use them day by day to get better. I am thankful for all of them.

Your Courage

When in doubt, do the courageous thing. That is a quote from a South African Prime Minister who faced many adversities in his life.

It is one of my favourites, because by choosing to do the courageous thing means that you have put yourself on the line and taken the initiative to step into the fray and face the fight head on. What a magnificent thing to do.

The amazing poet John Donne says in one of his very special poems, "Do not go gently into the night but rage, rage, rage with all your might." While he was speaking about dying, I feel that every time we let a situation or circumstance beat us, we are dying a little each and every time. Do not let life beat you. It is not out to beat you, it is out to forge your metal in the steel of fire. Rage, fight and do what you have to, to forge a good future for yourself.

You cannot do this by being a mouse. Be a lion – roar at the injustice life has dealt you and then learn to roar at life. It is not going to beat you. It is not going to be the winner. You are. You are going to find your courage, your strength and your fortitude and you are going to rage at life and beat every challenge that is thrown at you.

You can only do this is you are courageous. Know your strengths and work to your strengths and be courageous in your life.

Rage against the night that threatens to overwhelm you. Rage against the night. Rage against what has been done to you and your family.

Then use that rage as fuel to move you forward, to plot and plan a future in which you are in control. Be the captain of your ship, the master of your fate.

Nelson Mandela of South Africa spent twenty-seven years in prison on Robben Island which sits in Table Bay near Cape Town. He was imprisoned for being a political activist. Twenty-seven years he sat on that island, chopping rocks. From there he could see Cape Town, and knew that his family were going about their lives, without him.

He knew that he was missing out on watching his children grow up, but he stuck to his convictions.

He raged against the injustice in which the government at the time was entrenched. He never gave up hope for a better future for himself and for all of South Africa.

After twenty-seven years he came out of prison as South Africa had changed its Apartheid laws. The nation voted for this man of conviction, this visionary, into power and he became President. He never let his circumstances overcome his passion. He kept his belief in a better future strong, and he succeeded, where, for almost three decades, he could easily have felt like a failure and let his circumstances overwhelm him.

I tell you this story as a lesson in not letting where you are now dictate where you will be if you hold strong to the belief that there is a better tomorrow.

Don't let other people dictate your life. Seek your own approval, as not everyone is in your life to hold you up and support you.

Be true to yourself, and to your faith. Be strong within yourself. Trust that you know what is intrinsically right for you.

I discovered that I had to stop seeking other people's approval, but instead be the first person to encourage myself. I then made myself a daily routine of looking myself in the mirror every morning and speaking positive words to myself.

I spoke words to myself such as:

"God loves you
You are loved
You are strong
You are beautiful

You are a great mother
You will make it
You can do it
Don't let anyone tell you otherwise
You are powerful
Do not stand in your way because the universe is here to reward you"

Those were my daily statements of affirmation.

After speaking positive energy into myself, I feel energized and ready to face the world.

It may sound trite, but it works. When you are feeling down and as if life is getting the better of you, give yourself a pep talk.

When I realised that my pep talks did work on me, I then repeated similar statements of affirmation to all my children one by one. This routine is very therapeutic and indeed it is working. By not allowing circumstance to be the victor, we have re-built and revived our confidence, and we are more courageous.

We are okay and we will be fine, because I am determined not to stop doing what I have to. I am determined not to stop searching, learning and implementing things in my life that give me the next stepping stone.

We don't always get to see the entire journey and the end, but we do get to see the next stepping stone, and for me that is enough.

I have courage, faith and the determination to succeed. I refuse to be victimised by life and I am going to succeed just as I know that you too can succeed if you make a committed determination to do so.

Have the courage to live your life to

the fullest and deal with whatever circumstance, situation and curve ball comes your way.

Those are detours, not your destination. Be strong, because you owe it to yourself to succeed.

Your Influence

Do not ever think that what you do or say is blown away in the wind. Your children listen and absorb everything you say and do.

Be a positive role model, use your influence for good and for the good of your children. Be the best you that you can possibly be. More than that, be better than you think you can. Stretch yourself daily, and watch how much you grow,

People always underestimate how much they influence people.

You influence not just your children, but all the people you come into contact with. For all you know they might be fighting their own battle.

What you do, your story, and your positive action towards a good future may change another person's life.

People have come to me and said that my strength and courage has inspired them. I have to admit to being somewhat surprised. Being strong, courageous and resilient is a daily challenge. It heartens me to hear this as it means that I project a bigger me than I often feel, and that inspires me to do more, be more and succeed. I am determined to succeed every day. For myself, for my children and for the life I know we deserve.

Influence is an odd thing, as you influence everyone around you, for good or for bad.

The very well-used quote of Mahatmas Ghandi is very true: "Be the change you want to see in the world. If you want to see happiness, be happiness, if you want to see calm, and peace, be calm and live in peace."

If you want your children to be strong, show them what being strong is about, no matter the adversity. Be the you that you want to be, no matter what you feel, no matter how down you feel, no matter how hopeless you think your situation is – be the person and live the life you want. You are influencing people every day, so make sure you project a positive influence, because it will enliven you to be a better, stronger and more resilient person.

Use your influence for good because wallowing in the bad is just going to bring yourself and others down. We all know that life is hard. It has times that are truly miserable and you can wallow in them, sure, but what good does that do you? What good does that do your children? How does that move you forward?

It doesn't, and it won't. The only change that happens is the change you make happen.

Be the change. Have the courage. Use your influence for good. Make a change. Believe in a better tomorrow and live. Above all else live. Be happy. And choose to succeed.

If you stay in the current situation you are the inevitable will occur. However, if you are courageous enough to step into the abyss of change, the possibilities of potential suddenly become an option.

Only by being brave enough to walk away, or to change your current situation will you open the door for possibilities to enter. One day you will look behind you and find that you opening the door, and being courageous enough to walk through it has motivated others to follow you that may not have been strong or courageous enough to be the first person to open that door.

Be strong, be courageous and be of good spirit and you will not fail.

Chapter 9
Don't Look for Mr Right. Look for Mr Right for You

You are not Miss Wrong

When I accepted my current partner as a part of my life, I did that with an open mind, without doubt, bias or prejudice. I was looking at myself from the perspective of "I have been through the fire and now I have come out of it."

I came into this relationship with the attitude of, "this is the real me, what you see is what you get. Take me as I am."

I had decided to do away with all of the guilt, and I was already on my road to recovery. Plus I was aware of my current situation and the progress that I had already made. I am currently speaking from a platform of being a work in progress, however I can only get better. We are very quick to blame ourselves. It is the human condition. Some things are simply not your fault, even if you are not blameless. Let me explain.

Everybody is carrying around baggage from their past. These emotional suitcases are filled with pain, distrust, anger, depression, feelings of being not good enough, feeling of being unloved, unsupported or misunderstood and judged. There are many things that fill people's emotional suitcases.

Some people have had the courage to open them up and sort through the contents, though.

They have let the light into the suitcase and are working through the contents and discarding those things that they have dealt with, and are dealing with the ones that they are in a place to deal with. By doing this, your emotional baggage becomes lighter. You can move on. each time you take something out of your emotional suitcase, deal with it and discard it. Your baggage becomes lighter and lighter.

There is nothing wrong with you. There is nothing wrong with me. Simply because we have emotional baggage, does not mean that there is something wrong with us.

Trust me when I tell you, apart from a very, very few enlightened individuals in the world, every single person has an emotional suitcase that they carry around with them. Some people just pretend they don't, but they do.

The only person you can change is yourself.

What rewarding work it is to start working on your baggage and discard items because you are at a place in which you can let go, forgive yourself, forgive others and throw that item of your past away.

Every time you discard a hurt from your past, your suitcase gets lighter and you can walk forward in life easier.

We often don't want to open up the emotional suitcase because we are afraid that the contents are going to knock our feet out from under us, as they did when the hurt happened.

You are not the same person you were then. You are reading this book because you are making changes in your life and becoming stronger, wiser and more determined than ever to succeed.

When you start going through the emotional hurts that you carry around, you will be amazed at how many you can simply discard as being dealt with. Dealing with things can be hard, but not dealing with them will keep you in one place as your emotional suitcase will be so heavy that you won't be able to move forward.

Say, for example, that you lost your house, your car, your job, and the man in your life turned out to be a creep. Fine. Bad things happen and there are bad people in the world. Let it go.

Find a new job, a new car, work towards buying a new house and make friends with yourself. You don't need a man to make you whole. Become whole first, and then the right man will come along.

Miss Independent

My current partner is always ready to help me as best as he can, however I feel that what I am looking for is within myself.

I can no longer look to another person as my salvation, my answers are within myself.

I am my salvation, I know myself better than anyone else, and I have what it takes to succeed.

I just have to pull out that superstar inside of me so that she can serve not only me, but everyone else around me.

The biggest lie that women believe is that they need a partner. Having a partner is lovely, as it gives you another adult to lean on and share with, but it is not the be all and end all of life.

I have seen so many women miss out on so many amazing opportunities in life because they are waiting for their knight in shining armour to come and save them. The truth is, they don't need saving from their lives. They need saving from themselves, and the only person who can save them is them.

No man or woman can fix what is broken inside you – only you can. Yes, there are amazing professionals who can help you and guide you towards finding your answers, but you still have to do the legwork. You still have to save yourself.

What a wonderful thing to work towards! Being emotionally, financially and mentally independent. There is so much freedom in it, as you can go into a relationship not looking for a partner to complete you, but to walk at your side with you.

This takes the pressure off of both of you. You are more likely to find a stable individual to partner with, if you are not looking for a saviour.

On this point, avoid looking for people you can rescue you. Don't start relationships with them. You can only work on yourself, and should your work influence other people to want to work on themselves, then well done you. You cannot save someone else whilst you are trying to save yourself. Women especially love to take on men with broken wings because we think we can fix them. That is their journey, not yours and as every woman knows, we have enough on our plates.

Coming together as a couple should be from mutual places, not from one person being a crutch to the other. If you go into a relationship needing a crutch, be it emotional or financial, you may not make the effort to grow and become independent. Or the flip side may occur, that you do grow and become independent, but then your entire relationship changes and the ground rules that you went into the relationship with become invalid, and the relationship has to change or it falls apart.

Become your own best friend first. Then you will draw the right person into your life. One who can walk at your side, and not have to carry you and your emotional suitcase.

Be Miss Independent and enjoy your life every day, because you have the chance to make every day a new start towards being a better, stronger you. Be determined in your actions, thoughts and beliefs and work towards being your own person.

Be a strong person who can flip open her emotional suitcase and rummage around in it and discard old pain and hurt because she is strong in herself, because she believes in herself, and because she is worth the work.

It Takes Two Tango

One of the things I have had to learn, and it has been a very hard lesson, is that it does take two to tango.

This means that while there are things that I have to let go of and forgive myself for. I am not responsible for another's actions. The flip side is that I have to take some of the blame and learn to forgive myself.

Nothing happens in a vacuum. Predators pick their prey and the prey doesn't always see the predators coming. People who are plotting to hurt you and your family are not going to show their true colours up front, as this would have you running away so fast that Usain Bolt couldn't catch you. What they do is put forward a persona that is good, kind, loving and someone that will entice you into a relationship with them.

It is only once they have you 'trapped,' be

it financially, emotionally - by taking away your self-confidence, or even physically abusing you to the point that your self-confidence is gone and you believe that you are worthless and useless and don't deserve a better life. Only then they have they laid the ground work to reveal their true selves.

This is where your responsibility comes in. Do not go into a relationship where you need something from the person. Do not give others power over you. Be strong within yourself – especially become emotionally strong – so that when someone tries to belittle you, or break you down, or take away your freedom so that they can control you, you are strong enough within yourself to say, "No! This is not right, I don't deserve this!" And then walk away.

No-one has the right to hurt you. Not with words, not with fists, not with control.

That is their problem. But if you are strong within yourself, it won't become your problem. The first time a man raises a fist to you and you stay with him because, like me, you think it was a one-off situation, you are telling him that you accept the new status quo. He becomes the predator and you the prey. THAT is where you have just engaged in a very damaging tango with a man that has thrown away his respect for you, and thrown away your respect for yourself right along with it.

Being caught by a predator once can happen. There are many very sly people out there who are masters of their evil game. Bad things happen, and you have to let go. Forgive yourself for not seeing who he really was.

Sociopaths and Psychopaths are very good at hiding their true selves and they spin a sticky web around their prey without the prey even noticing they are slowly being trapped, until it is too late for them to escape.

I can tell you that you can escape. You have to escape. And you have to do it sooner rather than later. The longer you stay, the stronger the predator's game is going to get, as he thinks he has you where he wants you – powerless and too emotionally broken to leave.

When I was still married to my first husband, the one who had inflicted domestic violence upon me repeatedly, next door was a lady who was experiencing the same situation as myself. As soon as our husbands left for work, she either came to my house or I went across to hers and our main conversation was always centred around our husbands who beat us.

As we talked every day, I became more

and more determined to get out of that situation by leaving my husband, which I eventually did. My neighbour did not leave her abusive husband. I remember looking back at her door when I was leaving, and thinking, "Should I call the police on behalf of my neighbour or should I not?"

I didn't, and to this day I have lived with the guilt of having not helped this lady, because sometimes I think that by now she could have been beaten to death.

When I left my husband, I was seated in a pool of blood and that is how I was picked up and taken to hospital. I did not return. Had I had the confidence then that I have now, I would have been able to save at least one woman from continuing to suffer domestic violence

It takes years to be able to accept our irresistibility for bad relationships, especially if we were the victims. But we do have to, or it will lie like a rock in your suitcase, and you will drag it around with you forever.

Accepting some responsibility means that you have to look at what you did or did not do that could have changed the situation. Learn that lesson and throw the blame away. Once you have had a good look at it, seen what you need to, learned what you must, you owe it to yourself to never put yourself in that situation again. If you have learned from the past, you will never have to walk the same path twice.

There is a warrior in all of us. We just sometimes forget to wake them. Or we don't feel we could wake them. Being Miss Independent means that your warrior is always dressed for battle, and ready to fight for you. I am not advocating that you become a self-absorbed right-fighter.

I am saying that the person who walks with a lion at their side, even if the lion never roars, is not going to run into trouble with other animals.

Chapter 10: Believe in Your Purpose

Clarify Your Priorities

In my later years after I had given birth to all my children, I decided to go back to university. This was while I was a full-time wife and mother, so I knew it wasn't going to be easy. But I also knew that it was something I wanted to do.

I threw myself into my studies, but on the day I fell over and broke my ankle, my view changed, and the resulting circumstances that came to light made it clear that my priorities at the time had to be my children, and not the pursuit of full-time university studies.

Sometimes we hear the inner voice but fail to listen to it. Sometimes we block that inner voice out completely. It is easy to do as it, nevertheless it always speaks quietly. Often we don't want to listen to it, because it is saying things that we don't want to hear. Taking time to learn to listen to your inner voice is a must if you want to grow and become a stronger, wiser you.

Did it take breaking an ankle to get me to finally listen to my inner voice? Was that life's desperate attempt to get my attention? I don't know, but what I do know is that it took that fall to get me to realise what my priorities were.

When I returned from hospital, I had gotten my priories straight and gave my children my full and undivided attention, which I still do to this day. I am not saying that every woman has to be a full-time mother, but this is what I needed to do for myself and my children. I needed to be there for them wholly and completely/ My focus needed to be on their well-being in order to help them heal, grow and become strong.

That was my purpose. You have to find yours as it is different for all people.

First of all, search for your purpose. It can only be found within yourself.

Ask yourself some questions;

- How do I find my passion?
- What should I do now?
- Where do I start?
- How do I know what am good at?

At the time, as I was recovering and letting my ankle heal, I realised that I had gotten things wrong so many times, that I needed a new approach to finding my purpose. I decided to ask myself many questions, after which I discovered that I was not going to find my passion in what I did, but rather in who I am and who I became during the search journey.

Working on yourself is the greatest work anyone will every do. There are no right or wrong answers, no single one-size-fits-all answer. You have to do the inner work and find your own answers. What I can tell you is how rewarding this process is, as you see just how much you evolve along the way.

Don't chase material wealth.

We mistakenly determine wealth as how much money you have in the bank, or what size house you own, or what you can buy. This is one of the greatest untruths in life.

Life is not about what you have, it is about who you are, how you respect yourself and others around you. True wealth is about all those things you cannot buy with money.

Wealth is within you. It is in knowledge, wisdom and understanding. Wealth is knowing that you are being the best you that you can be. Wealth can mean that you were more patient today than you were yesterday. Wealth can mean that you finally took your children on that picnic you've been promising them. Wealth can be hearing yourself laugh and knowing it has been a while since you heard the sound. Look no further – wealth is inside you.

Oprah Winfrey once said that, "…having a closet full of great shoes was a great thing, but one would never live a fulfilled life just from possessing material things."

Her idea is, one needs to live a life of substance in order to live a fulfilled life.

You need to live a life that involves being true to yourself, through the offering of your entire self by living a life of service. That can be accomplished through showing compassion for other people, expressing commitment and constructive engagement with others. It comes from making the best out of every day, no matter the circumstances around you.

Greatness is determined through giving service to others. Greatness is determined by moving forward and creating a good future for yourself and your family.

Greatness is determined by helping yourself to become strong so that you can help your children become strong. When you do this, when you work on these things daily. your life will unfold with such beauty and grace.

Money cannot buy happiness. Money cannot buy respect, nor hope nor dreams. That all comes from a resonation of your inner wealth and sharing of your inner wealth with others. This idea resonates very well with me.

Failure is Part of the Experience

What doesn't kill you makes you stronger. We all say that, but part of what makes it is a cliché' is that it is also very true. Every failure in my life has been a stepping stone to an opportunity.

I may not have been able to see that at the time, but I can see that now. I have not yet encountered a failure that has not progressed me to the next level of my higher self. Embrace failure and learn life lessons from it.

Failure is going to happen. Bad things are going to happen. You can't change that but you can change how you deal with it, and what your attitude is towards it. We are all going to get knocked down, but you only fail if you don't get up again. And again. And again. Learn the lesson, get up and move on.

Don't let failure be your epitaph. Failure is not having succeeded. Everyone can succeed if they just don't give up. Try, try and try again until you succeed. The only difference is your attitude and determination to succeed.

No matter the past, no matter the present, the future is always yours for the taking.

Get up and get going. Failure is a detour. Get back on the road to success. Never give up and you will succeed.

Appreciate the Journey.

My philosophy has always been and will always be this: the past is gone the future is not here yet and all I have is the present. Therefore, I have learned to value and make good use of the here and now.

I have learned to live in the moment. I appreciate every new day for the gift it is.

The journey is always interesting.

Maya Angelo once advised Oprah to fill every moment with love, because on this journey of life we build our lives every day with every life we touch.

We influence every person we come into contact with, so choose to be a good influence.

Choose to appreciate today, to appreciate the people you have in your life that love you. Appreciate where you are and how far you have come. And most of all, appreciate the opportunities that still lie ahead of you for growth and experience.

Live your life. Live it to the fullest and always, always be grateful for what you have.

It's time to become the success you want to be.

Your future is in your hands. Look after it, treat it with respect and go forward with your head held high. Let no man steal your joy and let no person tell you that you are not valuable and precious. You deserve happiness. Fight for it.

Do what you have to in order to make peace with your past, so that you can move on to a glorious future.

Chapter 11:
It's Time to Become the Success that You Want to Be

Invest in your Self Education

The day I decided to invest in my self-education, was the moment my million-dollar question was answered. My question was that: What is your passion? Being able to answer that and making the changes necessary to work on that, was the most gratifying decision that I have ever made and the best money I have every spent. I say this without a shadow of a doubt. For the first time in my life, I felt liberated, in control and knew that my future was in my hands. I came to believe in the power to control my life.

Sometimes the answers need to be shown to you. I was fortunate enough to find an understanding and knowledgeable life coach. I had been following my current coach online for a while, but because I had already listened to and had been following several other online motivational speakers and coaches, I was not quite convinced that I should work with him. Nevertheless, I continued following him religiously, as was the norm at the time for me, but this time I stayed until the end of the presentation.

He gave an invitation to the audience as he always did: email him if they needed to write a book and change their lives. I did just that.

If I can say that being the Christian that I am, my first best decision was to accept Jesus Christ as my personal saviour in my life, then please allow me to confess that having met Geoffrey Semaganda and starting to work with him was the second best decision I have ever made in my life. I have grown tremendously along this life journey, and my life will never be the same again. I do attribute a huge part of my success to him. Thank God I met him. Working with him has given me tools to use in my life, and helped me find my inner strength.

While you can do the inner work on your own, I do advocate reaching out to a professional for help. They are emotionally distant enough to be able to help you without becoming bound by your situation as you are.

They are trained to see things holistically. Everyone knows that when you are dealing with pain, that pain becomes your focus. Often you can't see past it. That is why having an outsider listening and coaching you is so important. They will help you see things in a bigger picture, and help you to find your answers.

The answers lie within you—all of them. But sometimes you need help finding the right tools to extract them. I am very grateful for my Coach and the path he has walked with me.

Have a Mentor

Even when you have found your passion and are working on it and towards your good future, it is important for a person to have a mentor to take them through the technical know-how of one's journey. Walking your path with a professional, builds trust and self-confidence in you, and shows you just how to be the best version of yourself through the mentoring sessions.

You don't have to do this alone. There are

many wonderful people out there who can help you and guide you. Ask around, look for the right person for you and get the help you need.

Professionals see things differently. They have heard your story before. I am not belittling what you are going through, I am just saying that they, more likely than not, will have dealt with the situation before and will have answers or suggestions for you that you may not have thought of. Take the leap of faith and allow your past hurt to be taken out of your suitcase so that it can be dealt with, and put aside.

There is no reason that you have to carry these hurts around with you forever. They will hold you back and stop you from moving towards your goals and your future.

Remember Jan Smuts' quote: "When in

doubt, do the courageous thing." Asking for help is going to be one of the hardest and most courageous things you will do for yourself. If will also be the most rewarding, so make the decision to get help and start on your new life, today.

Have a product to sell

In my case, my product is me. I have a story to tell, that will help others who are going through, or have been through similar salutations.

I have learned to speak up about what I am passionate about and what I believe in.

If my story and this book can help one other person, my work has been a success. Life gives us good and bad, but we can use both to help others. Isn't that really what we are here for? Not to amass monetary wealth, or material possessions, but to enrich our lives by enriching other people's lives.

Know your story, know your product and get out there and sell it. By giving of yourself to others, you will heal. By giving of yourself to others you will help other people by being an example. I am my product, and my story is my product. What I have learned along my often difficult path is my product, and I trust that it will help others in their lives, whatever stage they are in.

Without a product, one is like a house without a foundation. You have to know what your foundation is. That is what you rest on and what supports you. It is on this foundation that you can build your future.

Build a business

There is nothing as fulfilling as building a business around your passion. Take Richard Branson for example, he built his entire empire around things that he was passionate about. He did not look for the best investment, or the one that was going to make him millions, he went after the things that sparked his interest, and that awoke his passion.

Living the life that you were created to live and doing what you love and enjoy doing, gives you a life of substance. If you can do what you love, you will never have to work a day in your life.

This means that because you are doing what you love, it will not feel like work, because every day will be filled with what you are passionate about. That cannot feel like work drudgery.

Give of your entire self through service to others, by doing the inner work and using that to teach and help others. Then use that to create a business, earning a living from it at the same time. That is the best way to live that I know. It makes what we have gone through seem as if it is being put to good use, and is not just a piece of my past that I wish never happened. It did happen. But the lessons I have learned from it have brought me to where I am today. For that, I have to be grateful as I am in the best position I have ever been in.

I have made peace with myself and my past and am using it to help others make peace with theirs.

I am using my past to create my future and in that way, I have been able to take all that pain and hurt out of my emotional suitcase.

I walk a better path because I am a better person and I work on that every single day because I am determined to not let the past hold me back from the future I know I deserve.

Chapter 12: Unstoppable Mother

Have Faith

Faith is the opening reference of everyone's first chapter of their future. It is the first step to take and nothing can be done without it. With faith all things are possible. In J.M. Barry's book Peter Pan, Wendy is afraid to fly and Peter says to her, "All you need is faith, trust and a sprinkle of fairy dust."

I like this because it sums up courage for me. You have to have faith that things are going to be okay.

You have to have trust in yourself that you are going to make a better life for yourself. And you have to have a sprinkling of fairy dust – which is a spot of belief in the impossible, and in the magic that is out there in life if you will just believe in the impossible.

Faith is believing in things unseen and trusting in the things that are not yet evident. Without faith you won't take the first step forward, into the abyss that the future can feel like. Trust that you deserve to walk towards a good future. Have faith that the universe is going to rally around you and bring people into your life to support and help you. And trust that there is magic in the world that comes to you in co-incidences, chance meetings and by taking the first step.

My Top Five Principals for Success

I have five top maxims that I believe in that I want to share with you. We have walked a long way together through this book, and I know that you are going to carry on making changes in your life that will lead you to where you want to be.

My five maxims are:

1. **Believe in yourself** and know that everything is possible if you have faith and work towards your goals. There is an abundance of success waiting for you, you just have to determine where you want to be and step boldly and without fear onto that path.

2. **Take responsibility** for all your actions and their possible outcomes.

    It becomes easier to learn you're your mistakes when you stop blaming others for them. No one is perfect and no one expects you to be perfect, so let go of trying to be and live fully.

3. **Take big risks.**

I believe that big risks give birth to big opportunities. A small step only gets you a small way forward, so take the risks. Take the big steps and step boldly into your future.

This is your life, rage against the dying of the light, rage against the night and be determined to succeed by doing the courageous things.

4. **Respond to fear positively.**

This is a scary one, but by not running from what you fear, but by instead embracing change, fear can and will push you to greater heights and help you grow. Keep going, no matter how bleak things look, as your breakthrough might just be around the corner.

5. Accept criticism

I never said these were going to be easy. Accepting criticism without taking offense is hard. Criticism comes from those who mean well, but will also come from those who mean you harm. Be discerning about who you accept criticism from, and learn to read people.

You will soon learn the difference between well-meaning criticism and just plain old mean criticism. Some people want others to fail as that is their way of lifting themselves up. It is horrible, but it is a harsh reality. So react to all criticism positively, objectively and with discernment.

Dorine's Final Golden Lesson

Lay your rules out clearly and stick to them, whether you are dealing with your children or other people in general. Set your boundaries for your children and for yourself. Do not let anyone steal your joy. Do not let anyone make you feel as if you are worthless. You are special and precious, and this is your life.

If I can overcome my past, I have every faith that you can too. Reach out and let others in. Don't let anyone step over your boundaries, as they are the walls within which you can grow, and nurture your growth. Be strong, be courageous, be passionate and above all, be determined to succeed.

Conclusion

As we have walked this journey together you will have seen that while I landed in some bad situations in my life, I found the determination within myself not to let them be my story. I have used my past to create my future, and to reach out to others with it. We all have a story to share. We all have faced challenges in our past, or maybe even in our present. But I want to tell you what you are not governed by your past.

You are the captain of your own ship. Choose life, choose to fight for your future, and believe in yourself and your ability to make a success of your life, from today onwards, and from this moment onwards.

You can choose to start now. With determination and faith you will succeed.

We are not what has happened to us. We are what we create out of what has happened to us. I refuse to let my past destroy my future. I am determined to succeed, and I hope that this book has inspired you to go forward and find your glorious future. You deserve one, so make it happen. Be strong, be discerning and be determined. The past is lost, but the future is yours to shape into the life you want to live. Start working on it today and soon you will look back and see that the life you dreamed of has come to fruition.

Don't ever give up, but get up and get going. Everyone can write their own story, their own future, just as I have.

Printed in Poland
by Amazon Fulfillment
Poland Sp. z o.o., Wrocław